THE RÉSUMÉ DOCTOR

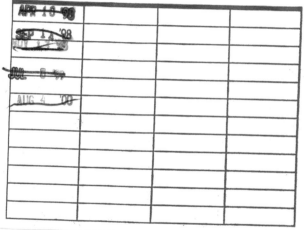

THE
RÉSUMÉ
DOCTOR

John J. Marcus

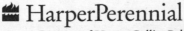

HarperPerennial
A Division of HarperCollins*Publishers*

HarperCollins books may be purchased for educational, business, or sales promotional use. For information, please write to: Special Markets Department, HarperCollins*Publishers*, Inc., 10 East 53rd Street, New York, New York 10022.

FIRST EDITION

Designed by Nancy Singer

Library of Congress Cataloging-in-Publication Data

Marcus, John J.
  The résumé doctor / John J. Marcus—1st ed.
    p. cm.
  Includes index.
  ISBN 0-06-273369-9
  (pb: alk. paper)
  1. Résumés (Employment)   I. Title.
HF5383.M26 1996
808'.06665—dc20   95-21631

96 96 97 98 99 00 ❖/HC 10 9 8 7 6 5 4 3 2 1

To Rosanna, whose life reads like a perfect résumé.

"The man who is prepared has his battle half fought."
—Cervantes, Don Quixote

CONTENTS

ACKNOWLEDGMENTS   xiii

PREFACE   xv

CHAPTER ONE—THE KEY COMPONENTS OF A RÉSUMÉ   1

The Purpose of Your Résumé   2
Job Objective   4
The Profile   7
Education   9
Work Experience   15

CHAPTER TWO—OVERCOMING PROBLEM AREAS   23

Number One: A History of Unrelated Positions   23
Number Two: Lacking the Experience That a Position
   Traditionally Requires   29
Number Three: Undergoing a Recent Decrease in Responsibility   34
Number Four: Having an Embarrassing Position on Your Résumé   40
Number Five: Having Several Periods of Unemployment in
   Your Work History   46
Number Six: A Record of Job-Hopping   52
Number Seven: Being Unemployed   58
Number Eight: Nearing Retirement Age   64
Drawbacks to the Functional Format   79

CHAPTER THREE—THE SECONDARY SECTIONS   81

Professional Organizations   81
Community Activities   82
Honors and Awards   83

Licenses and Certifications   84
Patents   84
Publications   84
Foreign Languages   85
Computer Skills   85
Part-Time Jobs and College Work Experience   86
Hobbies and Interests   86
Military Experience   86
Personal Data   88

CHAPTER FOUR—PUTTING IT ALL TOGETHER   89

The First Draft   90
The Chronological Format   91
The Functional Format   96
Things to Avoid   97
Résumé Length   101
Résumé Appearance   110

CHAPTER FIVE—SPECIAL TIPS, SPECIAL SITUATIONS,
AND SPECIAL JOB HUNTERS   116

Special Tips   116
  The Profile   116
     Convey Multiple Strengths   117
     Convey Qualifications for a Diverse Job Objective   119
     Highlight Key Background Information   123
     Highlight Early Work Experience   127
     Highlight Important Personal Qualities   130
  The Objective/Profile Combination   132

Special Situations   134
  Honors and Awards   134
  The Fact That You've Been Recruited   137
  Letters of Recommendation   140
  Customers' Comments   142
  Untraditional Statements   144
  Personal Information   149
  Prestigious Companies   151
  A Progression of Increasingly Responsible Positions   154
  Repetitive Positions   157

Special Job Hunters   161
  The Career Changer   161
     When to Highlight Your Education and Not Your Work Experience 161
     When to Highlight Your Key Skills and Strengths   163

When to Highlight Volunteer and Community Activities 165
Career Change and Concealing Your Age 170
The "Partial" Career Changer 173
The Graduating Student 179
The Housewife Reentering the Work Force 183

CHAPTER SIX—COVER LETTERS 187

Cover Letter for an Unsolicited Résumé 188
Composing the Cover Letter 188
Cover Letter for Responding to Newspaper Ads 196
Cover Letter for Contacting Executive Search Firms 199
Cover Letter for Contacting Employment Agencies 201
Cover Letters for Networking 201

CHAPTER SEVEN—THE RÉSUMÉ-LETTER 204

Analysis of the Résumé-Letter and How to Compose It 206
Success-Rate of the Résumé-Letter 208

CHAPTER EIGHT—WHERE TO GO WITH YOUR RÉSUMÉ 210

Personal Contacts 210
Editors of Newsletters 211
Prospective Employers 212
Companies Advertising Job Openings 214
Professional Organizations 214
Executive Search Firms 214
Employment Agencies 216
Résumé Databases 216
On-Line Job-Listing Services 218

INDEX 219

ACKNOWLEDGMENTS

Many thanks and much appreciation to Robert Wilson, my editor at HarperCollins, for his immediate enthusiasm for this project and constant support throughout.

Deep gratitude also to all of my résumé clients, who inspired me to write this book and from whom I never stop learning.

And my appreciation and love to Laurie, my wife and best friend, who so often answers before I knock.

PREFACE

I entered the employment business in September 1968. My career has included performing contingency recruiting for Fortune 500 companies, executive search work, outplacement counseling, and career counseling in Los Angeles, San Francisco, Boston, and Sarasota, Florida.

For the past fifteen years, I've concentrated on career counseling. I assist clients in determining the best position to pursue and how to get the right interviews, then convert them into offers. One of my key services is creating an outstanding résumé.

Obviously, I've written an enormous number of résumés. Throughout the years, I've heard the same plea time and again from a wide variety of clients:

"John," they tell me, "I'm really good at what I do, but my background has a few problems in it. I'm much better at my work than my résumé reads. If I could only get the right interviews, I know I could get the offer I'm looking for. Can you fix my résumé so I look as strong as I really am?"

I give my clients exactly what they want, and there's nothing fancy, tricky, or complicated about it.

How I turn a troublesome work history into a terrific, honest résumé is what *The Résumé Doctor* is all about. My goal is to teach you—someone who's seeking interviews and offers—how to write a résumé that you'll be proud of . . . one that will give you confidence as a job hunter and, more important, enable you to land the position you want.

The Résumé Doctor is of value to everyone, regardless of their level of seniority or personal circumstances—the first-time job seeker, the individual in midcareer, the person seeking to make a career change, the job hunter pursuing advancement in the same field, and the housewife desiring to enter or return to the work force.

To avoid awkwardness, I've written this book using masculine pronouns. The content pertains equally, of course, to men and women.

When referring to prospective employers, I often use the word *company*. It applies to any kind of organization that could possibly hire you—organizations such as a business, an educational institution, a medical practice or facility, a law firm, a social services or charitable organization, or the government.

I wish you the best of luck with your résumé and your search for employment. I hope you have as much success in finding the position you want as I have had enjoyment in writing *The Résumé Doctor* for you.

CHAPTER 1

THE KEY COMPONENTS OF A RÉSUMÉ

Fantastic! The manager you want to interview with just picked up your résumé. You really want this job! Okay, he's reading your résumé. . . . Hey, what went wrong? He just glanced at it—no more than 10 to 15 seconds—then tossed it in the reject pile.

What happened? You thought you had a great shot at that job because you have the right experience.

Well, I'll tell you what happened: a land mine in your background just exploded and shattered your chances of getting the interview.

If you're not setting up the appointments you want and expect, then your résumé probably has something in it that's working against you and turning interviewers off.

When employers initially read résumés, they look for reasons *not* to interview people as much as reasons *to* interview them. In a mere 10 to 15 seconds, they decide whether to put the résumé in the reject pile or to consider it further.

One major negative point can eliminate a candidate who has the exact experience an employer is looking for. The fact that so many people have problem areas in their background is one reason why companies invite in for interviews only one applicant for every 245 résumés that they receive!

Some job hunters are aware that there's a glaring shortcoming in their background. Others are not. Regardless of which group you fall into, wouldn't you like to know how to evaluate your background and résumé with a new, trained eye? Wouldn't you like to be able to write your résumé so it doesn't work against you? Isn't it time your résumé stopped acting as your own worst enemy?

1

In *The Résumé Doctor*, you'll learn what the eight biggest problem areas are to guard against. You'll know how to eliminate them from your résumé or minimize the impact they have on prospective employers. In addition, you'll learn how to showcase your strengths and successes so that your capability jumps off the page.

The net result will be that your résumé will give people every reason to interview you and no reason to pass you by. You will enjoy new confidence about your background and abilities as a job hunter, generate a maximum number of interviews, and feel more relaxed and self-assured when being evaluated by prospective employers. As a result, you'll land the job you want.

Now that you know where you'll end up after having read *The Résumé Doctor*, let's start at the beginning to see how to get there.

THE PURPOSE OF YOUR RÉSUMÉ

Your résumé has only one purpose: to present your qualifications in such a convincing way that prospective employers arrange interviews with you. Your résumé isn't supposed to be your life story and tell employers everything about you. Instead, its mission is to concentrate on the work part of your life and enable you to get the interviews you want.

If you know what kind of work you want to do, then your résumé will highlight the most relevant parts of your experience and convey your capability in that area.

If you don't have a particular position in mind and are wide open to a variety of jobs, then you'll describe your greatest strengths and achievements in order to demonstrate your ability to hold a number of different positions.

In both of these cases, however, you'll be delving into your background and deciding what it is that you want to emphasize about yourself on your résumé.

From a résumé-writing standpoint, your *background* consists of the work you may have decided you want to do plus all the different areas in your life experience that could possibly contain important information for employers to have about you. These include your:

Job Objective

Education

Professional Work Experience

Professional Organizations

Community Activities

Volunteer Positions

Part-time Jobs

College Work Experience

Honors and Awards

Licenses

Certifications

Inventions and Patents

Publications

Foreign Languages

Computer Skills

Hobbies and Interests

Military Experience

Personal Data

These parts of your background form the different sections of your résumé. They are its building blocks, and each section contains a specific type of information about you. (There's actually one more section that's called a "Profile." This section summarizes your background and takes information from the other sections. It will be discussed in detail shortly.)

With the vast majority of job hunters, the most important sections are their objective, profile, education, and work experience. These are the key component parts of the résumé, and they are used the most often and comprise the lion's share of the information that employers are looking for when deciding whether or not to interview people. Many job hunters, in fact, are able to write an excellent résumé using these four sections alone.

The other sections, if used at all, perform the role of rounding out a background and providing additional data when it will help to advance someone's qualifications. With some job hunters, such as the graduating student, the individual leaving the military, and the person seeking a career change, these other sections can be extremely important and will sometimes contain the bulk of the information in their résumé. Chapter Five offers important information for these types of individuals.

Let's now discuss how to present your job objective, profile, education, and work experience.

JOB OBJECTIVE

There's enormous disagreement among employment professionals as to whether or not a résumé should state a job objective. A decade or two ago this wasn't the case. This statement was as much a part of a résumé as was the job hunter's name, address, and telephone number.

Throughout the 1990's, however, many career advisors have been telling job hunters to omit an objective from their résumé. Their argument is that this statement limits the types of positions for which someone can be considered. Instead of opening doors, it closes them. Their preference is to begin a résumé with a profile. This will enable employers to get an idea of the different types of work the individual is capable of performing, thus increasing the likelihood of being invited in for interviews.

The camp in favor of including a job objective, however, feels that the absence of this statement can lead people to believe that an applicant is without career direction and will take any job he can get. After all, employers are always telling people that they want to hire goal-directed, motivated individuals. What better way is there to demonstrate that you're this type of person than by beginning your résumé by stating a specific job objective?

For example, imagine the impact it would have on a manager who has run an ad for a "Senior Test Engineer" when he receives a résumé that begins with "Objective: Senior Test Engineer." This applicant is clearly going to get off to a strong start and have his résumé read with enthusiasm. (The opponents of declaring a job objective contend that job hunters can explain their career goals in the cover letter that accompanies their résumé. The fact of the matter is that it's much more convincing when this statement appears on the résumé itself, instead of being typed in a letter that's being custom-tailored in response to an ad.)

Those in favor of stating a job objective also believe that an effective way to offset the possibility of this statement's closing doors and reducing opportunities is to have two or three résumés, where each one is written for a specific kind of position and contains a different job objective. While this approach will certainly be effective for answering ads (you send the résumé that's the best fit for the advertised position), it won't be as useful for conducting a mass-mailing of your background. Can you imagine how people at a company would react if they received three résumés from you, each one stating an interest in a different type of position?

Clearly, there's no "right" way to handle this matter of the job objective. Here's how to proceed, depending on your individual situation.

If you're interested in doing a specific kind of work, then state this as your job objective.

If you're open to a variety of positions, you have three choices. First, you can write a special résumé for each position, where each résumé states a different job objective. Second, if the positions you're interested in are closely related, you can use one résumé that states all of these positions in the objective. A third possibility is not to use an objective at all, and, instead, begin your résumé with a profile.

If you don't know what kind of work you want to do, you'll be better off not stating an objective and beginning your résumé with a profile.

WORDING YOUR OBJECTIVE

What you say in your objective can range from as little as just stating the title of the position you're seeking, to including information on the kind of organization you want to join and the industry it's in. It just depends on how specific your goal is. Two important factors to keep in mind are (1) how qualified you are for the position you're seeking, and (2) how available this job is. The stronger your qualifications and the greater the job's availability, the more specific you can afford to be when wording your objective. If you don't have strong credentials for the position you want or the job is in short supply, then you had better word your objective loosely so that you don't limit your opportunities.

Here are a number of job objectives to review. Notice that some are very specific, while others are not. Some specify the type of employer that's desired; others note the types of positions that the job hunter is interested in. One objective even mentions the work setting that's desired, while another specifies the importance of having good promotional opportunities. The purpose of listing all these objectives is to show you the wide range you have when stating your employment goal.

Flight Attendant.

A challenging position in Infection Control or related services.

Fitness Counselor, working in a corporate environment.

Chef or Sous Chef at a fine-dining restaurant, country club, or resort hotel.

In-house Counsel at a real estate title company, financial institution, or industrial corporation.

Registered Nurse working in a critical-care setting, with the goal of progressing into a management responsibility.

Applications Engineering or Product Management position with a growing producer of electronic or electro-mechanical products.

Professor of Science Education at a college or community college.

A challenging position in Marketing Support or Office Administration, providing extensive interaction with coworkers, customers, and suppliers.

Senior Graphic Designer at a television station or corporation with an in-house art department.

A commission-based Outside Sales position with a manufacturer or distributor of specialty chemicals.

Management position at a psychiatric hospital, mental-health clinic, or family-counseling center, responsible for Staff Supervision and Training, Staff Education, or Quality Assurance.

General Manager of a full-service restaurant, Director of Field Operations for a restaurant chain, or Corporate Staff position in Food & Beverage, Training, or Marketing.

Vice President-Manufacturing for a multiplant producer of textile products.

President of a bank with assets in excess of $1 billion dollars.

When composing your job objective, be sure you never make statements like these:

A position that offers recognition and advancement in exchange for loyalty and diligent effort.

A challenging position that offers growth potential and the opportunity to utilize my experience and expertise.

A rewarding, problem-solving position that draws upon my skills and presents the opportunity for professional advancement.

Although these job objectives explain what someone is looking for in the larger sense of the word, they're so broad and general that they basically say nothing. Many employers also interpret objectives like these to mean that the job hunter has no idea of what he wants to do and will accept any position he can get. If you can't be any more specific than making statements like the above, omit an objective from your résumé and use a profile.

There's one instance when stating a broad job objective is acceptable. It's when someone has just completed their studies and is looking for an entry-level position to begin their career. Here, employers don't disapprove when they learn that someone's goal is little more than to find a position that will make use of the academic training they just completed. Following are recommended objectives for recent graduates:

An entry-level position that will effectively utilize my educational background.

An entry-level position where my training in ———— will be utilized effectively.

A challenging entry-level position in ————, providing the opportunity to utilize my educational background and skills in ————.

An entry-level position in the ———— field, providing the opportunity to utilize my related education and build a career.

An entry-level position where I can learn a field and build a career, with the goal of progressing into a management responsibility.

THE PROFILE

As already mentioned, if you don't know what kind of work you want to do or if you want to expose yourself to a wide variety of positions, you'll be better off beginning your résumé with a profile instead of an objective.

This statement that summarizes your career usually ranges from two to four sentences in length. It details your key areas of expertise and may also include one or two significant achievements along with important personal traits.

What a profile does is highlight your capability and make an immediate and highly favorable impression on prospective employers, prompting them to read your résumé in its entirety. Once they have done so, they can decide where you might fit in at their company.

A profile is frequently preferred by senior-level job hunters, due to their depth and breadth of experience and the different positions they are able to perform as a result.

Here are some examples of profiles to review to see the variety of information that can be included in them:

11 years' experience in Health Club Sales and Management. The winner of more club and personal sales contests than any individual in the chain—signed up over 10,000 new members in the last 5 years. Created new programs and dramatically improved quality and efficiency of facilities. An excellent trainer, manager, and motivator of personnel.

An accomplished attorney with extensive administrative and technical experience in land-title insurance and real-estate appraisals and closings. The author of numerous real-estate articles and opinions published by national, state, and local newspapers and professional organizations, including the *American Bar Journal, Chicago Tribune,* and newsletter of the Illinois Bar Association.

An Information Systems Executive with 22 years' progressively responsible experience. Currently managing a $6,500,000 budget and 65 employees in a 960-bed hospital. Offer a blend of management expertise and leadership with information systems acquisition, design, development, and implementation.

A diversified medical/business background that includes performing public-relations activities for small companies as well as being a Cardiopulmonary Perfusionist on Dr. Michael D. DeBakey's heart team in Houston, TX. Extensive experience doing business with doctors and executive-level personnel at hospitals and HMOs. After successful rehabilitation from open-heart surgery, completed the New York Marathon in 1990. Frequently give informational and motivational talks before the American Heart Association.

Over 12 years' experience in all phases of Retail Management with a history of producing dramatic increases in revenues and profits—most recently boosting a store's sales 50% in 6 months. An expert in opening new locations, improving product mix, creating and instituting new services for customers, plus analyzing under-performing units and implementing effective solutions to get sales and profits back on track.

An innovative consumer-packaged-goods Sales Executive with P&L responsibility plus a history of increasing revenues, profits, and market share while decreasing costs. Strengths include Sales Management of Direct Forces and Broker Networks, Development of National Accounts (drug stores, mass merchandisers, and food stores), and Organizational Restructuring and Development. An energetic and goal-directed leader.

An M.B.A. and C.P.A. with an outstanding record of results in Management and Financial/Business Analysis. Produced dramatic increases in sales and profits, most recently turning around a company that had lost money each of the previous 4 years. Highly imaginative and resourceful—a continuous generator of new ideas.

A Senior Financial Executive with both Big 6 and international, multi-unit manufacturing experience. Strengths include strategic planning, MIS, acquisitions and divestitures, cost reduction, and tax and audit. A history of increasing revenues and operating efficiencies while reducing costs.

While you're expected to give an enthusiastic presentation of your strengths and accomplishments in a profile, be sure you're never verbose or overuse adjectives and superlatives. Avoid describing yourself as in the following, where nothing specific is said, but a lot of clichés and hype are used:

PROFILE   A dynamic, self-motivated, results-oriented, shirtsleeves Manager who is proficient in creatively motivating staff members to achieve goals that far surpass objectives established by Top Management.

When employers receive résumés containing a profile like the above, they seldom have an interest in meeting the applicant.

A profile can also be used for purposes other than to substitute for a job objective. These are discussed in Chapter Five.

Other names you can use for this section are "Summary," "Career Summary," and "Summary of Qualifications."

EDUCATION

This section presents information on your educational background. An important consideration with this section is where to place it in your résumé.

If the work you want to perform requires a specific degree or degrees—as do the teaching profession, the law profession, and most medical and mental-health positions, for example—then present your educational background just before you discuss your work experience. As an illustration, here's the résumé of a dentist. This job hunter wants to close down his private practice and join an insurance company, working in its claims department.

John D. Gross, D.M.D.
10 Morris St.
Sarasota, FL 34232
(813) 377-7694

OBJECTIVE   Dental Consultant with an insurance company, responsible for reviewing dental insurance claims, assessing their accuracy, and determining the extent of benefits.

EDUCATION   D.M.D., University of Louisville School of Dentistry, 1966.
B.S., Science and Pre-Dentistry, University of Louisville, 1963.

Licensed in Florida and Kentucky.

EXPERIENCE   PRIVATE PRACTICE: Sarasota, FL (1990–present), Tampa, FL (1985–1990), Livermore, KY (1971–1985), and Louisville, KY (1968–1971).

• Practice general dentistry with significant exposure to prosthodontics, endodontics, periodontics, pedodontics, and oral surgery.

• Handle up to 100 patient visits per week and as few as 25, the latter when scheduling a number of patients requiring comprehensive treatment with extended appointments.

• Established each of these practices and employed staffs consisting of a chair-side assistant, hygienist, and receptionist.

• Instituted a preventive dentistry program in Livermore, KY, by successfully influencing the township to put fluoride in the water system.

• Continuously maintain an excess of required CEUs.

ORGANIZATIONS American Dental Association.
Florida Dental Association.
West Coast Dental Association.
Sarasota County Dental Association.

References furnished on request.

If a specific educational background isn't required for your career choice, then describe your education toward the end of your résumé. This will allow you to get right to your work experience and the heart of your qualifications.

Here are the different ways to list your education depending on the amount that you have.

If you have an advanced degree, state this degree along with your undergraduate degree:

EDUCATION   M.A., Art History, University of North Carolina, Chapel Hill, NC. 1993.

B.A., Art History, State University of New York, Buffalo, NY. 1991.

If you're currently pursuing an advanced degree but haven't received it yet, give your current educational training plus the four-year degree that you have:

EDUCATION   M.S. Program, Advanced Registered Nurse Practitioner. Will receive degree from University of South Florida in May 1997.

B.S., Nursing, University of Tampa, 1995.

If you have only an undergraduate degree:

EDUCATION   B.A., Accounting, University of South Florida, Tampa, FL. 1992.

If you're currently pursuing your undergraduate degree, or a two-year degree from a community college, but haven't received it yet:

EDUCATION   B.S., Social Work, New York University. Will receive degree in May 1997.

or

EDUCATION   A.S., Pilot Technology, Manatee Community College, Bradenton, FL. Will receive degree in Fall 1996.

If you have only a two-year degree from a community college:

EDUCATION   A.S., Physical Sciences, Hillsborough Community College, Tampa, FL. 1992.

If you have just a high school diploma:

EDUCATION   Diploma, Antioch High School, Antioch, TN. 1977.

If you have college or community college experience and lack a degree and also don't plan on completing your studies:

EDUCATION   Rollins College, Winter Park, FL. 1990–1992.
Concentration in Accounting and Economics.

or

EDUCATION   Manatee Community College, Bradenton, FL. 1988–1991.
Studied Liberal Arts.

If the type of work you do requires only a certificate:

EDUCATION   Certificate, Hairstyling, Manatee Area Vo-Tech, Bradenton, FL.
1972.

If your only post-high-school educational experience is taking work-related courses or attending lectures and seminars, list these programs. Here's the educational background of a quality assurance supervisor in the electronics industry:

EDUCATION   Naval Weapons Center, China Lake, CA. 1985–1991.
Certified annually at this Military Defense Instructors Course.

Staff Motivation, National Institute of Business Management,
1994.

Coaching Skills for Managers & Supervisors, Fred Pryor
Seminars, Tampa, FL. 1994.

Files and Records Organization, Padgett-Thompson Seminars,
Tampa, FL. 1994.

Customer Service, Fred Pryor Seminars, Tampa, FL. 1994.

Diploma, Coral Gables High School, Coral Gables, FL. 1978.

If your only post-high-school educational training is attending company-sponsored courses, state them. Here's what a store supervisor working for Payless Shoe Stores put down:

EDUCATION   Attended numerous Payless Corporate seminars and workshops in Advanced Management Techniques. Subjects included: Selecting and Interviewing Candidates, Public Speaking, Maintaining Store Standards, Coaching and Counseling Sales Associates, and Financial Controls.

Diploma, Gainesville High School, Gainesville, FL. 1985.

If you have a college degree, or even an advanced degree, and also have additional educational training that pertains to your field, include this information when you feel it will enhance your credentials.

Here's how an insurance executive described his education that included course work after receiving his college degree:

EDUCATION Currently studying to obtain C.I.C. designation, with property and casualty portions completed.

Industry-related courses at The College of Insurance, including Business Law and Accounting. 1971–1973.

Numerous Management courses at Princeton University, 1972.

B.S., Business Administration, New York University, 1969.

And here's what a sales manager wrote:

EDUCATION B.S., Business Management, Villanova University, Villanova, PA. 1985.

Attended Xerox Sales School and Xerox Management School, Cleveland, OH. 1986.

When discussing your educational background, don't include any courses or schooling that are unrelated to your line of work.

All that stating these programs will do is draw employers' attention away from the education that you want them to be focusing on.

Last, if you have a four-year degree, you don't need to include a two-year degree (if you happen to have one). Likewise, if you have a two-year degree, omit the high school you attended.

Along with your course work, major, and degree, there are other matters to consider when presenting your educational background: your grade point average (G.P.A.), extracurricular activities, honors and awards, and the fact that you may have paid for a significant portion of your schooling.

As far as your G.P.A. is concerned, include it only if it was 3.50 or higher. For example:

EDUCATION M.A., Education, Lynchburg College, Lynchburg, VA. 1992. G.P.A. 3.70.

> B.A., Economics, Randolph Macon Woman's College, Lynchburg, VA. 1991.
>
> G.P.A. 3.65.

When deciding whether or not to state your G.P.A., you should also take into consideration how important your degree is in your field and how long ago you were graduated from college.

The more recent your educational experience, the more relevant it will be.

Extracurricular activities that pertain to your line of work can also be important and are appropriate in your résumé. Here's what someone wrote who wanted to go into either the public relations field or the advertising business:

EDUCATION B.A., Communications, University of Arkansas, 1993.

> Member, Public Relations Society.
> Committee for the Restoration of "Old Main."
> Staff writer and copy editor for college newspaper.
> Member, Debate Club.

Again, you need to consider how much weight prospective employers will place on your participation in these activities and how many years you have been out of school.

Academic honors and awards are always impressive. They will distinguish you as a student during your college years. As a general rule, include them regardless of how long it's been since you were graduated. For example:

EDUCATION B.A., Economics, Denison University, Granville, OH. 1972.

> Cum Laude.
> Recipient of Lewis Newton Thomas Scholarship.

Last, there's the matter of having paid for a significant portion of your educational expenses. Having "worked your way through school" demonstrates great motivation and seriousness of purpose, two factors that always make a favorable impression on employers.

If you're a graduating student or recently completed your education, always include this information. For example:

EDUCATION B.A., Finance, Florida State University, 1995.

> Paid for 75% of education through working summers and holding part-time jobs during the school year.

WORK EXPERIENCE

We now come to the part of the résumé that's the longest and most important section for the majority of job hunters, the one that discusses their work experience. (There are two exceptions: the recent college graduate and the individual who is making a career change. Here, other aspects of a background will often be more important than the work that's been performed to date.) Work experience usually comprises 75 to 95 percent of a résumé. In fact, when most people talk about their résumé, what they're really referring to is the information that appears in this section.

Work experience can be presented in two different ways: the *chronological* format or the *functional* format.

The chronological approach is used more widely and most job hunters automatically opt for it, so I'm going to discuss it first. In addition, you can't appreciate the advantages of the functional format unless you understand the disadvantages of the chronological. Once you understand the benefits and drawbacks of each of these approaches, you'll be able to decide which one to use.

In the chronological résumé, work experience is presented in reverse chronological order, starting with the current or most recent employer, then working backwards. With each employer, the following information is given: the organization's name, its location by city and state, the dates of employment, the type of business the organization is in, and then the job hunter's job title (or job titles, when there have been promotions), followed by a listing of key responsibilities, duties, and accomplishments.

Here's an example of a résumé that uses the chronological format for the "Experience" section:

Gary R. Sevitch
3544 Almay Ave.
Sarasota, FL 34239
(813) 955-3860

OBJECTIVE   General Manager of a growing retail business, preferably selling home furnishings and furniture.

EXPERIENCE   **GARSON'S, INC.**, Sarasota, FL. 1990–present.

Company is a furniture retailer with annual sales of $5,000,000.

General Manager with complete responsibility for P&L, Sales, Purchasing, Merchandising, Advertising/Sales Promotion, and Administration.

- Increased profits 72% in 4 years.
- Upgraded and modernized the showroom.
- Revamped purchasing department and instituted new vendors.
- Created traffic-producing advertising and sales-promotion programs.
- Implemented effective incentive programs for sales staff.

DECORAMA, Bradenton, FL. 1985–1990.

Sales Manager for this retailer of furniture and home furnishings. Annual sales: $3,000,000.

- Increased sales an average of 20% per year over a 5-year period.
- Recruited, hired, trained, and motivated a sales staff of 6.
- Conducted training sessions on new products as well as on effective sales and closing techniques.
- Created successful print-, radio-, and television-advertising campaigns.

GULF COAST HOME FURNISHINGS, Sarasota, FL. 1978–1985.

Assistant Sales Manager at this $1,000,000 retailer of curtains, draperies, and bedspreads.

- #1 sales producer—consistently exceeded quota.
- Interviewed potential Sales Associates and helped train new hires.
- Assisted Sales Manager with merchandising, displays, and advertising/sales-promotion programs.

CONNIE'S CURTAINS, Venice, FL. 1976–1978.

Sales Associate for this retailer of curtains and draperies.

EDUCATION   A.A., Manatee Community College, Bradenton, FL. 1976.

This chronological résumé shows a job hunter who has enjoyed an extremely successful career as a retailer in the home furnishings and furniture businesses. Gary Sevitch worked his way up from a sales associate to an assistant sales manager to a sales manager and now to general manager. Each of his job changes was for more responsibility with a company in the same field. Each position served as a springboard for the next.

This chronological presentation is an excellent way to discuss your background so long as it consists of an uninterrupted progression of growth in your field, as is the case with Gary. Because of the way the résumé is laid out—especially the prominent placement of titles—it will emphasize your growth from one company to the next.

If you happen to have worked for one organization for an extended period of time and have had a series of promotions, the chronological format will highlight these successes as well. The résumé of Lee Bermant demonstrates this:

Lee Bermant
4625 Las Brisas
Sarasota, FL 34238
(813) 923-8333

OBJECTIVE

General Manager of a full-service restaurant.

EXPERIENCE

THE GULF SHORES, Sarasota, FL. 1979–present.

Restaurant is a seafood establishment employing 50 people and seating 200 diners.

General Manager-1989–present. Complete responsibility for all operations including marketing, accounting, and administration. Direct 6 managers.

- Changed image of restaurant and implemented marketing programs that increased revenues 25% within 6 months.
- Revamped key departments and instituted changes throughout restaurant, producing a 12% reduction in operating expenses.
- Automated the business office.
- Personally contract for all services, select vendors, and perform the purchasing.

Assistant to General Manager-1987–1989.

- Scheduled, trained, and supervised 45 wait, kitchen, and bar personnel.
- Monitored food quality and waste.
- Visited diners at tables to ensure customer satisfaction. Also resolved any problems customers were experiencing.
- Greeted diners upon entering and leaving restaurant.

Bar Manager-1984–1987.

- Trained bartenders.
- Scheduled and supervised personnel.
- Performed inventory control of liquor, fruit, and mixers.

Bartender-1981–1984. **Waiter**-1979–1981.

EDUCATION

Diploma, Sarasota High School, 1976.

References furnished on request.

We see that Lee joined The Gulf Shores restaurant as a waiter and worked his way up through bartender, bar manager, assistant to the general manager, then to general manager. Again, the chronological format brings out this consistent progression of growth.

Clearly, the chronological approach is excellent for describing experience if you have an unblemished background like Gary Sevitch and Lee Bermant. However, if you're like the millions of job hunters who have one or more of the following problem areas in their background,

- A history of unrelated positions
- Lacking the experience that a position traditionally requires (but you know you have the ability to do the job)
- Undergoing a recent decrease in responsibility
- Having an embarrassing position on your résumé (one that's contrary to your career path)
- Having several periods of unemployment in your work history
- A record of job-hopping
- Being unemployed
- Nearing retirement age

then the chronological format won't work for you. This is because of its structure. Due to the prominent placement of *titles* and *dates of employment*, it will place as much emphasis on *when* you did something as it will on *what* you did. As a result, these problem areas will be conspicuous.

In order to generate the interviews you want, you need to present your work experience in a way that will highlight your strengths and accomplishments without any regard to the time period in which they occurred. The way to achieve this is through describing your work experience in the *functional* format. In this type of résumé, instead of presenting your responsibilities, accomplishments, and duties in reverse chronological order by employer, you explain what you've done according to job function, or type of work performed. You group your related successes together regardless of which company they occurred at. Then, at the end of the résumé, under a section titled "Employment History," you list in reverse chronological order the names of your employers, their locations, and dates of employment. Including job titles is optional.

Here's an example of a résumé that uses the functional format for the "Experience" section:

Henry C. Layton
936 Concord St.
Sarasota, FL 34231
(813) 923-3621

OBJECTIVE

An executive-level Sales/Marketing position with P&L responsibility.

EXPERIENCE

Management

- Founded and built an advertising agency that billed over $1,000,000 the first 9 months of being in business.
- Creative Director for a $10,000,000 direct-mail company. Managed 43 employees in 6 departments, including graphics, creative, cash order, mailing, advertising, and catalog sales.

Direct Mail

- Conceived of a technique to increase direct-mail response that became an industry standard. Generated responses as high as 20%. Mailings included letters, brochures, catalogs, and stand-alone pieces.
- Created a system to continually develop a targeted mail audience that resulted in millions of dollars in sales.
- Developed a system to key direct mail that saved 20% in processing costs.

Media Advertising

- Managed advertising budgets in excess of $1,000,000.
- Created and conducted a campaign that increased business 200% within 1 year.
- Developed a series of ads that was so successful that future promotions were canceled due to an excess of prospects.
- Decreased advertising production costs by 25% at a $10,000,000 dealer of stamps and coins.
- Other marketing campaigns included the development and use of slide/video programs, audiotapes, brochures, instruction manuals, catalogs, and newsletters.

Additional Duties

- Produced and edited a video that generated over $500,000 in new business.

- Established and conducted a nationwide seminar series that increased sales of a department's products 100% the first year. Potential customers also paid a fee to attend these seminars, resulting in a new profit center for company.

- Secured front-page articles about a company's product line in major trade publications.

- Managed trade shows, including design of display material, set up of booths, and supervision of booth personnel.

- Wrote speeches for civic groups, business associations, and trade organizations.

- Produced multimedia presentations for the real-estate industry. Also pioneered the use of slide/video programs, which have become an industry standard.

- Published a "Florida" specialty magazine. Built circulation within a 2-county area to 30,000 within 2 years.

- Recruited, hired, and trained a sales force that doubled revenues within 18 months.

EDUCATION

M.B.A., Northeastern University, 1969.

B.A., Business Administration, Boston University, 1967.

EMPLOYMENT HISTORY

Automation Corporation, Sarasota, FL. 1990–1995.
Second Opinion Home Inspection, Sarasota, FL. 1989.
Advantage Publishing, Sarasota, FL. 1986–1987.
Independent Marketing Consultant, Sarasota, FL. 1984–1986.
MKT Associates, Inc., Sarasota, FL. 1982–1984.
Royal Stamp & Coin Co., Inc., Manchester, NH. 1969–1980.

References furnished on request.

As you can see, this résumé does an outstanding job in emphasizing Henry Layton's strengths in management, direct mail, and media advertising, due to the way the document is laid out.

Let's now look at the backgrounds of eight job hunters, each of whom must contend with one of the problem areas just cited. You'll see how the chronological format brings out a deficiency in each case. The functional approach either completely eliminates the problem area or greatly minimizes the impact it will have on prospective employers.

Again, this is the result of getting readers to focus on *what* someone has done instead of *when* they performed the work and *with which employer*.

CHAPTER 2

OVERCOMING PROBLEM AREAS

NUMBER ONE: A HISTORY OF UNRELATED POSITIONS

Like many people, Les Kelley has moved back and forth between jobs in different fields. He's currently selling real estate, after a stint selling wine, and now wants to return to restaurant management, his first professional position.

Les has outstanding experience in the restaurant business, with an impressive slate of accomplishments. In his chronological résumé, however, these successes are offset by his having left the field (two times, in fact) and gone into other lines of work.

Due to this bouncing back and forth, many employers who review Les's background will stop midway and set his résumé aside. They'll feel that they might get one or two good years out of him, but then Les will just pick up and leave, probably to go into outside sales once again. There's not much incentive to bring him in for an interview.

Les's chronological résumé depicts him as an extremely capable individual—in the restaurant business as well as in other fields—but unstable and a high-risk candidate for long-term employment. Here's his résumé:

Les Kelley
4655 Chamis Way
Sarasota, FL 34235
(813) 378-1784

OBJECTIVE   General Manager of a full-service restaurant.

EXPERIENCE   TROY ASSOCIATES, Sarasota, FL. 1995–present.

Realtor for this real-estate broker.

- Member of "Million Dollar Plus Club."
- Recipient of "New Associate Achievement Award" for Southwest Florida.
- Developed a specific service area the first year with company and became #1 real-estate agent in this marketplace.

WINE COUNTRY IMPORTS, Troy, MI. 1992–1995.

Sales Representative for this importer of fine wines.

- Opened up new market for wine sales: restaurants and hotels.
- Tripled territory revenues in 3 years.

BRICK ALLEY BISTRO, Detroit, MI. 1986–1992.

General Manager of this casual/creative-dining restaurant seating 200 people. Directed 80 employees including 6 managers.

- Increased revenues 125% in 6 years and developed the facility into a three-star restaurant.
- Performed all the recruiting, hiring, training, and scheduling of personnel.
- Created and implemented staff-training programs, plus conducted sales and service seminars on a regular basis to ensure consistently high quality standards.
- Designed effective marketing programs and promotional materials, along with handling public and media relations.
- Contracted for all outside services, selected vendors, plus purchased required equipment, furniture, fixtures, and supplies.
- Oversaw administrative operations, and personally handled payroll, tax deposits, plus maintenance of personnel records.

Les Kelley
Page 2

ADVANCED FOOD PRODUCTS, Sarasota, FL. 1984–1986.

Regional Director for this manufacturer of a new quality-assurance product for the food-service industry.

- Called on restaurants, hotels, and contract feeders in a 9-state area.
- Brought many prospective customers to the testing stage, including Hilton Hotels, Walt Disney World, General Mills Restaurants, and TGI Friday's.

COCA-COLA BOTTLING COMPANY OF FLORIDA, Sarasota, FL. 1982–1984.

Account Representative, responsible for the sale of Coca-Cola products.

- #1 producer in territory for bringing in new accounts.
- Increased sales 40% the first 6 months.

HISTORIC HOLLY HALL, Holly, MI. 1979–1982.

General Manager of this upscale fine-dining restaurant seating 200 people. Directed 50 employees including 4 managers.

- The first outside manager to operate the facility, increased revenues 50% in this 3-year period.
- Changed image of restaurant and rewrote the policies, procedures, and the operational manuals.
- Established effective cost-and inventory-control systems.
- Directed food, dining, marketing, administrative, and financial activities.

THE COW PALACE, Sarasota, FL. 1972–1979.

Restaurant was a steak house that employed 40 people and seated 160 diners.

Assistant General Manager-1976–1979.

Bar Manager-1974–1976.

Bartender and Waiter-1972–1974.

EDUCATION   Diploma, Coral Gables High School, Coral Gables, FL. 1969.

References furnished on request.

Now here's Les's functional résumé, which I call the "Consolidator." What it does is blend Les's several restaurant management jobs under one category, "Restaurant-Management Background," and spell out loud and clear his expertise in not only managing restaurants, but in instituting significant changes at them and dramatically increasing their business. In the Consolidator, Les's entire career, including his sales experience, now directly relates to his chosen field, the restaurant business.

After reading Les's functional résumé, there's every reason to interview him for a restaurant-management position, and no reason not to. Just look at his track record in managing restaurants and marketing products to them.

Les Kelley
4655 Chamis Way
Sarasota, FL 34235
(813) 378-1784

OBJECTIVE

General Manager of a full-service restaurant.

RESTAURANT-MANAGEMENT BACKGROUND

- Complete responsibility for managing restaurants seating up to 200 diners and employing up to 80 people with 6 managers. Facilities included casual/creative-dining, upscale fine-dining and seafood.

- Increased revenues as much as 125% in a 6-year period of time.

- Changed a restaurant's image and developed it into a three-star facility.

- Rewrote policies, procedures, and operational manuals.

- Performed all recruiting, hiring, training, and scheduling of personnel.

- Developed and implemented staff-training programs, plus conducted sales and service seminars on a regular basis to ensure consistently high quality standards.

- Established cost-and inventory-control systems.

- Created effective marketing programs and promotional materials, along with handling public and media relations.

- Contracted for all outside services, selected vendors, plus purchased required equipment, furniture, fixtures, and supplies.

- Oversaw administrative operations, and personally handled payroll, tax deposits, plus maintenance of personnel records.

FOOD-SERVICE/WINE-SALES EXPERIENCE

Regional Director for a manufacturer of a new, state-of-the-art quality-assurance product for the food-service industry.

- Called on restaurants, hotels, and contract feeders in a 9-state area.

- Brought many prospective customers to the testing stage, including Hilton Hotels, Walt Disney World, General Mills Restaurants, and TGI Friday's.

Les Kelley
Page 2

Sales Representative for a wine importer.

• Opened up new market for wine sales: restaurants and hotels.

• Tripled territory revenues in 3 years.

EDUCATION

Diploma, Coral Gables High School, Coral Gables, FL. 1969.

EMPLOYMENT HISTORY

Troy Associates, Sarasota, FL. 1995–present.
Wine Country Imports, Troy, MI. 1992–1995.
Brick Alley Bistro, Detroit, MI. 1986–1992.
Advanced Food Products, Sarasota, FL. 1984–1986.
Coca-Cola Bottling Company of Florida, Sarasota, FL. 1982–1984.
Historic Holly Hall, Holly, MI. 1979–1982.
The Cow Palace, Sarasota, FL. 1972–1979.

References furnished on request.

NUMBER TWO: LACKING THE EXPERIENCE THAT A POSITION TRADITIONALLY REQUIRES

Today, an ever-increasing number of people want to change careers and perform work that they've never done before. Often, they have the ability to handle the new position, but they lack the experience that the position traditionally requires. Their chronological résumé brings out this deficiency, since their current or last job has little to do with the field they want to enter.

Let's take the case of Alexa Brookline. In her chronological résumé, Alexa's objective states that she wants to go into outside sales and sell art supplies. But she's been teaching American history for the past 10 years! A manufacturer or distributor of art supplies has no reason whatsoever to interview Alexa. Few, in fact, will read her background past her position at the Venice Middle School. Here's her résumé:

Alexa Brookline
5339 Lake Place Blvd.
Sarasota, FL 34233
(813) 925-4007

OBJECTIVE Outside Sales Representative for a rapidly growing manufacturer or distributor of art supplies.

EXPERIENCE SARASOTA MIDDLE SCHOOL, Sarasota, FL. 1989–present.

American History Teacher. Complete responsibility for the eighth-grade American History course.

- Plan the curriculum, establish daily objectives, determine length and sequencing of topics, select teaching materials, and teach the class.
- Design, administer, and grade tests, plus write progress reports on each student.
- Enforce rules for classroom conduct, supervise extracurricular activities, and plan and conduct fund-raising events.

VENICE MIDDLE SCHOOL, Venice, FL. 1987–1989.

American History Teacher.

- Planned and taught the American History course to eighth grade students.
- Performed testing, wrote student evaluations, and supervised extracurricular and fund-raising activities.

THE NOKOMIS SCHOOL, Nokomis, FL. 1986–1987.

Art Teacher.

- Established the Art Department for this private elementary school.
- Specified necessary equipment and supplies, and designed layout of art room.
- Interviewed, evaluated, and selected vendors, negotiated pricing, and coordinated contract preparation with bookkeeper.
- Designed curriculum and instructed students in painting, drawing, and sculpture. Materials used included watercolors, finger paints, oils, acrylics, colored pencils and chalks, crayons, charcoal, clay, plasteline, as well as modeling tools, paint brushes, kilns, glazes, easels, canvases, and paper.

Alexa Brookline
Page 2

HERBALIFE INTERNATIONAL, Sarasota, FL. 1986.

Sales Representative.

• Sold dietary and nutritional products to Sarasota residents.

• #1 salesperson in the district.

• Performed extensive prospecting and generation of referrals.

• Achieved highest average number of weekly presentations: 30.

• Held best closing ratio: 50%.

• Attained highest rate of referrals: 85%.

SELBY PUBLIC LIBRARY, Sarasota, FL. 1985–1986.

Library Assistant.

• Conducted the Saturday Afternoon Children's Hour.

• Visited elementary schools to read stories to students.

• Prepared materials for children's programs and assisted the Youth Librarian in the acquisition of new books.

EDUCATION   M.Ed., Social Studies, University of South Florida, 1984.

B.A., Art Education, University of South Florida, 1982.

References furnished on request.

Now here's Alexa's functional résumé, the type I call the "Magnet." It pulls out from her work history the two areas that directly pertain to her job objective: an extensive knowledge of art supplies and successful experience as an outside sales representative.

Notice that Alexa used the headings "Art-Supplies Background" and "Sales Experience" for discussing these two parts of her work history. Whereas her talents in these areas are buried in her chronological résumé, they're prominent in the Magnet. Also notice that instead of calling this section "Experience," Alexa titled it "Qualifications," to underscore the fact that she has the skills that are needed to perform her job objective.

In the Magnet, Alexa no longer looks like a schoolteacher. She looks like someone eminently qualified to sell art supplies.

Alexa Brookline
5339 Lake Place Blvd.
Sarasota, FL. 34233
(813) 925-4007

OBJECTIVE

Outside Sales Representative for a rapidly growing manufacturer or distributor of art supplies.

QUALIFICATIONS

Art-Supplies Background

Complete responsibility for establishing the Art Department at a middle school.

- Specified the required equipment and supplies.
- Designed layout of art room.
- Interviewed, evaluated, and selected vendors.
- Negotiated pricing and coordinated contract preparation with bookkeeper.
- Designed the curriculum and instructed students in the use of equipment and materials. Supplies included water colors, finger paints, oils, acrylics, colored pencils and chalks, crayons, charcoal, clay, plasteline, modeling tools, paint brushes, kilns, glaces, easels, canvasses, and paper.

Sales Experience

Sold dietary and nutritional products in the Sarasota area.

- #1 Sales Representative in the district.
- Performed extensive cold calling plus generation of referrals.
- Achieved highest average number of weekly presentations: 30.
- Held best closing ratio: 50%.
- Attained highest rate of referrals: 85%.

EDUCATION

M.Ed., Social Studies, University of South Florida, 1984.
B.A., Art Education, University of South Florida, 1982.

EMPLOYMENT HISTORY

Sarasota Middle School, Sarasota, FL. 1989–present.
Venice Middle School, Venice, FL. 1987–1989.
The Nokomis School, Nokomis, FL. 1986–1987.
Herbalife International, Sarasota, FL. 1986.
Selby Public Library, Sarasota, FL. 1985–1986.

References furnished on request.

NUMBER THREE: UNDERGOING A RECENT DECREASE IN RESPONSIBILITY

Due to a series of family problems that started about ten years ago, Paul Antonelli got side-tracked and his brilliant career in the insurance business deteriorated. Paul went from managing a $14,000,00 budget and 400 people at Paramount Insurance to overseeing 25 people with a $3,500,000 budget at Cromwell & Associates. Then he became an insurance salesman at a small insurance agency.

Paul's chronological résumé resembles a bell curve. It depicts him as an executive who has topped out—even worse, declined. A company would be hard-pressed to interview him for an executive-level position.

Paul Antonelli
5654 Fredericks Way
Sarasota, FL 34243
(813) 351-5650

OBJECTIVE

A position with Profit & Loss Responsibility in Risk Management or a Senior Management post responsible for Developing and Marketing Insurance Products.

EXPERIENCE

PROGRESSIVE INSURANCE ASSOCIATES, Sarasota, FL. 1991–present.

Senior Agent at this full-lines insurance broker.

- #1 producer in the company, responsible for the sale of commercial and personal insurance.
- Perform extensive prospecting plus generation of referrals.
- Call on owners and managers of businesses as well as individuals.

U.S. FUNDING CORPORATION, Huntington Station, NY. 1988–1991.

Senior Producer/Assistant Manager for this mortgage bank.

- #1 producer out of 20 each year with company.
- Originated $3,000,000 to $5,000,000 of mortgages per month.
- Recruited, trained, and supervised new sales representatives.
- Assisted Manager in all administrative functions.

CROMWELL & ASSOCIATES, Chicago, IL. 1986–1988.

Regional Manager/Producer for this insurance broker. #1 producer out of 35 nationwide, with an annual book of $1,700,000.

- Put the company into the self-insurance business. Developed the products and accounts and brought in several Fortune 100 clients. Also developed Loss Control Programs for accounts.
- Personally produced 20% of all workers' compensation 29.01 programs in the state of Illinois.
- Directed a production/administrative staff of 25, with a $3,500,000 budget.
- Trained and developed branch-office personnel.
- Spoke extensively throughout the state on insurance and self-insurance issues.

PARAMOUNT INSURANCE COMPANY, New York, NY. 1981–1986.

Director of Risk Management for this full-lines stock-insurance company. Generated a $3,000,000 profit the first year, while Top Management was projecting a $5,000,000 loss. Built profit to $16,000,000 within 4 years. Administered a $14,000,000 budget and directed 400 employees.

- Established and built this department that provided self-insurance programs and services to client companies. Opened branch offices in San Francisco, Los Angeles, Dallas, Chicago, and Atlanta. Performed all staffing and training.

- Directed the solicitation, evaluation, and control of all programs and created the guidelines for production of new business.

ARGO-RISK MANAGEMENT, New York, NY. 1976–1981.

Midwestern Regional Manager for this full-lines stock-insurance company. Managed an administrative staff of 12 and a $2,000,000 budget.

- The only producer in the region and #1 producer in the company out of 800 nationwide. Grew business from $34,000,000 to $274,000,000 in 2 years.

- Directed a network of brokers/agents plus contacted organizations directly to achieve projected market penetration. Personally presented proposals to all prospective clients and followed through to close.

- Created many new products that became industry standards.

Originally joined company as **Account Executive**.

FRANKLIN ASSOCIATES, New York, NY. 1973–1976.

Account Executive for this insurance broker.

GRAHAM & ASSOCIATES, New York, NY. 1969–1973.

Account Executive with this insurance broker.

EDUCATION

B.S., Business Administration, New York University, 1969.

References furnished on request.

Now here's Paul's functional résumé, which I call the "Stabilizer." It portrays Paul as a seasoned professional in the risk management/insurance field, with a long history of generating impressive profits for his employers. Whereas the chronological format emphasizes Paul's career peak then slide, the Stabilizer smooths out his work history, combining achievements from his various positions. In the Stabilizer, Paul looks like a topflight insurance executive—as a manager, a producer of new business, plus a developer of new insurance products.

With family matters resolved, Paul is energized, and is now ready to resume his earlier flourishing insurance career. The Stabilizer will pave the way.

Paul Antonelli
5654 Fredericks Way
Sarasota, FL 34243
(813) 351-5650

OBJECTIVE

A position with Profit & Loss Responsibility in Risk Management or a Senior Management post responsible for Developing and Marketing Insurance Products.

RISK-MANAGEMENT BACKGROUND

Director of Risk Management:

- Established and built a Risk Management Department to provide self-insurance programs and services to client companies. Administered a $14,000,000 budget.

- Generated a $3,000,000 profit the first year in business, while Top Management was projecting a $5,000,000 loss. Built profit to $16,000,000 within 4 years.

- Opened branch offices in San Francisco, Los Angeles, Dallas, Chicago, and Atlanta and performed all the staffing and training. Responsible for 400 employees.

- Directed the solicitation, evaluation, and control of all programs and created the guidelines for production of new business.

Midwestern Regional Manager

- Inherited a $34,000,000 territory and grew it to $274,000,000 in 2 years. Managed an administrative staff of 12 and a $2,000,000 budget.

- Directed a network of brokers/agents plus contacted organizations directly to achieve projected market penetration. Personally presented proposals to all prospective clients and followed through to close.

- Created many new products that became industry standards.

Regional Manager/Producer

- Put a company into the self-insurance business, personally developing all the products.

- Created Loss Control Programs for consulting clients.

- Directed a production/administrative staff of 25, with a $3,500,000 budget.

- Performed extensive training of branch-office personnel.

- Spoke extensively throughout the state of Illinois on insurance and self-insurance issues.

Paul Antonelli
Page 2

INSURANCE-SALES EXPERIENCE

- #1 producer in the country with each employer—one employer had an 800-person sales force.

- Generated $274,000,000 worth of business in 1 year. The territory produced only $34,000,000 2 years previously.

- Developed all the accounts for a company new to the self-insurance business.

- Produced 20% of all workers' compensation 29.01 programs in the state of Illinois.

- Created feasibility studies for clients.

NEW PRODUCT DEVELOPMENT

- Met with clients and prospective clients, assessed their needs and created new products to meet their specifications.

- New products included: Dread-Disease Coverage
  Zero-Balance Accounts
  Mortgage-Assurance Plans
  Rent-A-Captive Programs
  Residual-Value Insurance
  Banking-Excess Programs

EDUCATION

B.S., Business Administration, New York University, 1969.

EMPLOYMENT HISTORY

Progressive Insurance Associates, Sarasota, FL. 1991–present.
U.S. Funding Corporation, Huntington Station, NY. 1988–1991.
Cromwell & Associates, Chicago, IL. 1986–1988.
Paramount Insurance Company, New York, NY. 1981–1986.
Argo-Risk Management, New York, NY. 1976–1981.
Franklin Associates, New York, NY. 1973–1976.
Graham & Associates, New York, NY. 1969–1973.

References furnished on request.

NUMBER FOUR: HAVING AN EMBARRASSING POSITION ON YOUR RÉSUMÉ

Some job hunters have one position in their background that's a source of embarrassment to them because it's so contrary to their career path. It's an obvious blemish on their résumé, and they wish it didn't have to be there. They consider omitting the position from the document, but this would just create an extended period of unemployment—equally embarrassing—in addition to being dishonest.

John Singleton was one of these individuals. He regretted the day that he decided to tend bar at the Hilton, needing to take some time off in order to figure out whether or not he wanted to stay in the sales field. Years later, he learned that this period of time on his chronological résumé would become a serious problem for him and require a great deal of explanation, regardless of his sales successes before and after tending bar.

Here's his résumé:

John R. Singleton
6 Pryor Rd.
Sarasota, FL 34242
(813) 349-9681

OBJECTIVE

A challenging outside sales position with the responsibility for bringing in new accounts plus expanding volume with existing customer base.

EXPERIENCE

GULF COAST HOSPITAL SUPPLY CORP., INC., Sarasota, FL. 1994–present.
Sales Representative.

- Sell procedure trays, disposable instruments, admission kits, and waste-management products.
- Call on doctors, nurse managers, and purchasing agents at hospitals on the Gulf Coast of Florida.
- Increased territory sales 50% in 2 years and achieved membership in Million Dollar Club both years with company.
- Personally conceived of a new product that is being reviewed by F.D.A. for approval.
- Member of a 3-person team that developed and packaged the Female Catheter Kit. Trained national sales force in marketing the product.
- Participated in the conception and development of a needleless anesthesia set. Product is awaiting F.D.A. approval.
- Manage a 7,500 sq. ft. warehouse—supervise 3 employees.

HILTON HOTELS, INC., Longboat Key, FL. 1992–1994.
Bartender.

MANASOTA ENERGY CORPORATION, Sarasota, FL. 1987–1992.
Marketing Representative.

- Sold windows, roofs, and siding to home owners.
- Performed extensive cold-calling and generated leads through referrals.
- Achieved average closing rate of 23%.
- Assisted Sales Manager in interviewing sales applicants.
- Participated in training new hires.

John R. Singleton
Page 2

BEST COMMUNITY DIRECTORIES, Falls Church, VA. 1985–1987.

Account Representative for this publisher of *Yellow Pages* directories.

- Sold *Yellow Pages* advertising to companies in Virginia, Maryland, and Washington, D.C.

- Generated over $1,000,000 of business a year.

- Performed extensive prospecting and closed over 80% of appointments.

- Consistently 1 of top 3 producers out of 60 in company.

- Member, President's Circle Club.

EDUCATION

B.A., Economics, University of Maryland, 1985.

References furnished on request.

Notice that John tried the best he could to make his bartender job as inconspicuous as possible. He put the names of his employers in capital letters with bold-face type and kept his titles in regular-face type with upper-and lower-case letters, not wanting to call attention to the word bartender. He also said nothing about his various responsibilities while tending bar, hoping that readers would concentrate on the positions he held before and after this job. Nevertheless, there it was—bartender—in black and white on his chronological résumé.

John's functional résumé, however, which I call the "Eliminator," solves this problem for him. It eliminates the bartender job from the document, and with no negative repercussions.

When John describes his work experience, he presents his sales accomplishments and duties according to the types of products and services he's sold. When he lists his employers in the "Employment History" section, he omits his titles. The embarrassing position of bartender does not even appear.

The Eliminator depicts John as an excellent salesman and an outstanding candidate for his job objective. Here's the résumé:

John R. Singleton
6 Pryor Rd.
Sarasota, FL 34242
(813) 349-9681

OBJECTIVE

A challenging outside sales position with the responsibility for bringing in new accounts plus expanding volume with existing customer base.

SALES EXPERIENCE

MEDICAL SUPPLIES

- Sold procedure trays, disposable instruments, admission kits, and waste-management products.
- Called on doctors, nurse managers, and purchasing agents at hospitals on the Gulf Coast of Florida.
- Increased territory sales 50% in 2 years and achieved membership in Million Dollar Club both years with company.
- Personally conceived of a new product that is being reviewed by the F.D.A. for approval.
- Member of a 3-person team that developed and packaged the Female Catheter Kit. Trained national sales force in marketing the product.
- Participated in the conception and development of a needleless anesthesia set. Product is awaiting F.D.A. approval.
- Managed a 7,500 sq. ft. warehouse—supervised 3 employees.

HOME-IMPROVEMENT PRODUCTS

- Sold windows, roofs, and siding to home owners.
- Performed extensive cold-calling and generated leads through referrals.
- Achieved average closing rate of 23%.
- Assisted Sales Manager in interviewing sales applicants.
- Participated in training new hires.

INTANGIBLE SALES

- Sold *Yellow Pages* advertising to companies in Virginia, Maryland, and Washington, D.C.
- Generated over $1,000,000 of business a year.
- Performed extensive prospecting and closed over 80% of appointments.
- Consistently 1 of top 3 producers out of 60 in company.
- Member, President's Circle Club.

John R. Singleton
Page 2

EDUCATION

B.A., Economics, University of Maryland, 1985.

EMPLOYMENT HISTORY

Gulf Coast Hospital Supply Corp., Inc., Sarasota, FL. 1994–present.
Hilton Hotels, Inc., Longboat Key, FL. 1992–1994.
Manasota Energy Corporation, Sarasota, FL. 1987–1992.
Best Community Directories, Falls Church, VA. 1985–1987.

References furnished on request.

The four problem areas that have been discussed so far have all concerned the kind of work that someone has done or has not done.

The next four problem areas pertain to the time sequence of someone's work activities. Either the person has had several periods of unemployment, has job-hopped, is currently unemployed, or is well on in years and nearing retirement age.

In each of these cases, the problem is caused by the dates of employment. What needs to be done is to minimize the effect that these dates will have on prospective employers. This is achieved by getting the reader to focus on the quality of work that's been performed and not on when the work was done or when the person was not working.

I call the functional format that will accomplish this goal the "Minimizer." In the pages that follow, you'll see the Minimizer at work helping to offset three of the four problem areas. The last one, "Nearing Retirement Age," cannot be handled by a résumé. Instead, job hunters must use what's known as a résumé-letter. This special type of letter is explained in Chapter Seven.

NUMBER FIVE: HAVING SEVERAL PERIODS OF UNEMPLOYMENT IN YOUR WORK HISTORY

A hurdle for many job hunters is having one or more extended periods of unemployment in their background. Employers get skittish when they see this on a résumé. The first two things that cross their mind are how competent the person is in their line of work and how committed they are to their profession.

Bob Keller is an accomplished production engineer, but his history of extended periods of unemployment makes getting interviews difficult. He was out of work between 1992 and 1994 and between 1986 and 1988. Upon learning this, many employers will file his résumé away and never even learn that Bob was also out of work between 1977 and 1979. Here's his chronological résumé:

Bob Keller
39 Green St.
Sarasota, FL 34235
(813) 377-5023

OBJECTIVE Senior Manufacturing Engineer, with the responsibility of developing and implementing state-of-the-art production processes and equipment.

EXPERIENCE HIBISCUS, INC., Tampa, FL. 1994–present.

Senior Production Engineer for this $30,000,000 company.

Hold technical and business responsibilities for all phases of R.F. heat-sealing operations from concept to shipment. Ship 1,000,000 units annually.

- Ensure that production levels are achieved according to schedule. Investigate stoppages and take appropriate action.
- Direct up to 25 personnel, including supervisors. Responsible for their training and safety.
- Designed and installed manufacturing equipment that increased production 100% while improving quality. Also designed production processes.
- Responsible for the handling, packaging, and storage of active dry chemicals in bulk to ensure compliance with OSHA and IOSH requirements.

ENGINEERED MATERIALS AND INSULATIONS and PROTEK ELECTRONICS, INC., Sarasota, FL. 1988–1992.

Senior Production Engineer at these two companies engaged in the potting, encapsulation, and electronic assembly of cables, harnesses, and circuit boards.

- Developed the processes, equipment, tooling, and molds required for production.
- Brought initial quality procedures, static controls, and chemical storage/handling to approved OSHA and mil-spec levels.
- Designed and implemented equipment for tabbing, staking, and material processing of battery assemblies.
- Recruited, hired, trained, and scheduled supervisors and technicians.

PRODUCTION RESOURCES, INC., Sarasota, FL. 1982–1986.

Principal of this consulting firm specializing in Production and Operations.

- Took a start-up company, Hyperpower, Inc., a producer of key (patented) power-supply assemblies for the medical and electronics industries, from an engineering prototype to over $1,000,000 in sales in less than 18 months.
- Designed the production processes, developed and installed tooling and fixtures, directed the purchase, installation, and implementation of production equipment, and selected and approved vendors and vendor tooling. Responsibilities also included layout, drag soldering, and component and wire prep.
- Trained and scheduled production personnel.

Bob Keller
Page 2

FAIRCHILD WESTON/SCHLUMBERGER (now LORAL DATA SYSTEMS), Sarasota, FL. 1979–1981.

Senior Production Engineer for this company that designed and manufactured flight and data recorders for government, commercial, and military users.

- Introduced new products into the electronics assembly area, including P.W.A.'s, component and wire prep, potting and encapsulation, and unit assembly to completion.
- Designed production machinery and processes, and trained and scheduled personnel.
- Increased recorder manufacturing output by 75%, while reducing costs 15%.
- Reduced time to release new products by over 70%.
- Approved tooling, equipment, and vendors.

SAXON/COPYSTATICS, INC., Miami, FL. 1977.

Manufacturing Engineer for this producer of photocopy equipment.
- Held engineering charge for main assembly line.
- Coordinated all "main line" product changeovers.

COMCO, INC., Miami, FL. 1976.

Mechanical Design Engineer for this company that designed and manufactured landmobile and aeronautical communications equipment.

EDUCATION　B.S. Manufacturing Technology, Indiana State University, 1976.

References furnished on request.

Now here's Bob's functional résumé, the first example of the "Minimizer."

This résumé accomplishes two things. First, because of its layout, it ensures that Bob's background will be read in its entirety; there's no reason to stop reading the document half-way through because no negatives appear. Second, because this résumé immediately makes such a strong case for Bob's capability, when the periods of unemployment do become apparent at the end of the document, they'll have a minimal effect on a reader.

Many employers will be so impressed with Bob's accomplishments and contributions that they'll want to meet him.

They'll be willing to wait until the time of the interview to find out the reasons for his having been out of work on several occasions. The résumé's primary purpose, to produce meetings with prospective employers, will have been achieved.

Notice that Bob inserted his titles in the "Employment History" section and used bold-faced type. These titles demonstrate continuity in his work background and also help to make the dates of employment less prominent.

Bob Keller
39 Green St.
Sarasota, FL 34235
(813) 377-5023

OBJECTIVE

Senior Manufacturing Engineer with the responsibility of developing and implementing state-of-the-art production processes and equipment.

EXPERIENCE

20+ years' experience performing manufacturing engineering for producers of high-volume electrical, electro-mechanical, and rubber products.

Management

- Took a start-up company producing power-supply subassemblies from an engineering prototype to over $1,000,000 in sales in less than 18 months.
- Directed up to 25 employees.
- Recruited, hired, trained, and scheduled supervisors, technicians, and production personnel.
- Created plant-safety programs that significantly reduced injuries and lost time. Ensured adherence by all employees.
- Wrote and implemented quality-control procedures, including training personnel in their use.

Manufacturing Engineering

- Devised production processes that increased manufacturing output by 75% and reduced costs by 15%.
- Reduced time to release new products by over 70%.
- Designed and installed manufacturing equipment that increased production 100% while improving quality.
- Sourced vendors and directed the purchase, installation, and implementation of production equipment.
- Designed production molds.
- Ensured that all production levels were achieved according to schedule. Investigated stoppages and took appropriate action.

Bob Keller
Page 2

EDUCATION

B.S., Manufacturing Technology, Indiana State University, 1976.

EMPLOYMENT HISTORY

Hibiscus, Inc., Tampa, FL. 1994–present. **Senior Production Engineer**.
Engineered Materials and Insulations; Protek Electronics, Inc., Sarasota, FL.
   1988–1992. **Senior Production Engineer**.
Production Resources, Inc., Sarasota, FL. 1982–1986. **Principal**.
Fairchild Weston/Schlumberger, Sarasota, FL. 1979–1981. **Senior Production**
   Engineer.
Saxon/Copystatics, Inc., Miami, FL. 1977. **Manufacturing Engineer**.
Comco, Inc., Miami, FL. 1976. **Mechanical Design Engineer**.

References furnished on request.

NUMBER SIX: A RECORD OF JOB-HOPPING

One of the problems that plagues job hunters the most is having a history of working for companies for only a short period of time. This is known as job-hopping.

With each successive move, it becomes that much more difficult to get interviews. As the number of jobs mounts, prospective employers become increasingly concerned that they'll become one more statistic in the job hunter's checkered past.

This is the case with Roy Givens. Roy has had six jobs in the last ten years, but, worse, four jobs in the last six. And he's looking to make a change once again! As soon as people see this job-hopping on his chronological résumé, they'll wonder what his problem is. Does Roy get fired from each position because of personality conflicts with management or his coworkers? Or does he become easily bored and just get up and leave? Few employers will want to meet him to find out.

Roy N. Givens
153 Gulf Ave.
Sarasota, FL 34236
(813) 366-7207

OBJECTIVE

A senior-level position in Marketing, Staff Training/Development, or Program Development/Management for a provider of health-care services.

EXPERIENCE

COMPREHENSIVE HEALTH SERVICES, INC., Sarasota, FL. 1995–present.

Manager of Provider Relations for this organization offering subacute and long-term medical care.

- Manage the marketing department, including staff training and development plus the creation and implementation of sales and marketing programs.

- Conduct extensive activities to cultivate referrals from accounts as well as from physicians and lawyers throughout the community.

- Perform market and competitive analysis, plus product development and enhancement.

NAPLES OUTPATIENT REHABILITATION CENTER, Naples, FL. 1994.

Case Coordinator/Recreation Therapist.

- Performed program development for individuals with head-injured, neurological disorders.

- Designed a life-skills curriculum, a social-skills curriculum, and cognitive and community reentry programs.

NEW MEDICO REHABILITATION OF FLORIDA, Wachula, FL. 1992–1994.

Supervisor of Training and Staff Development.

- Performed curriculum development for interdisciplinary professionals as well as physical, occupational, and speech therapists assisting patients with head-injured, neurological disorders.

- Recruited, hired, and trained paraprofessionals to work with patients, plus developed recruitment and internship programs to attract physical, occupational, and speech therapists. Also spoke at area schools and universities to develop job applicants.

- Created and conducted education courses in first aid, CPR, AIDS education, crisis prevention and intervention, CARF and HRS regulations, personnel/employee management, time management, workers' compensation issues/risk management, as well as general policies and procedures.

HUTCHINGS PSYCHIATRIC CENTER/PARKSIDE PSYCHOSOCIAL CENTER,
Syracuse, NY. 1992.

Program Director.

- Oversaw a $100,000 budget and a 10-person interdisciplinary team responsible for delivering vocational-rehabilitative, community reentry, and medical-management services to psychiatric, head-injured, and developmentally disabled patients. Performed case coordination from admission to discharge. Also performed program evaluation and quality assurance.

- Created and instituted 6-week modules for rehabilitation activities, and designed and taught community reentry and ADL classes on an individual and group basis.

- Performed community education through creating and conducting seminars on psychiatric illness. Additionally, gave marketing presentations on television, and designed, wrote, and produced brochures and manuals for client and family resources.

RESEARCH FOUNDATION OF THE STATE UNIVERSITY OF NEW YORK, Syracuse, NY. 1989–1991.

Support Services Coordinator.

- Recruited, trained, and supervised over 150 volunteers who provided medical, legal, housing, and counseling services for HIV and AIDS survivors and their families.

- Performed case management for over 40 people with AIDS/HIV infection.

- Created, taught, and coordinated AIDS-education courses for physician interns, community forums, and school systems. Also designed, developed, and negotiated the use of the first AIDS-education curriculum at the Auburn State Prison.

- Performed marketing activities on AIDS education as well as fund-raising for AIDS survivors.

KRAMER PSYCHIATRIC CENTER, Albany, NY. 1986–1989.

Recreation Therapist.

- Developed curricula for individual and group activities, including motor coordination, expression therapies, and arts and crafts. Population consisted of adolescents, adults, and geriatrics.

EDUCATION

B.S., Education, New York University. 1985.

References furnished on request.

Here's Roy's functional résumé, with the Minimizer in action. Just as this format helped Bob Keller with his periods of unemployment, it will help Roy minimize the fact that he has job-hopped. Before employers will even learn about this part of his work record, they'll see how talented Roy is in his field. Many people will be willing to disregard Roy's shortcoming and will set up interviews with him.

Roy N. Givens
153 Gulf Ave.
Sarasota, FL 34236
(813) 366-7207

OBJECTIVE

A senior-level position in Marketing, Staff Training/Development, or Program Development/Management for a provider of health-care services.

EXPERIENCE

Marketing

- Managed a health-care provider's marketing department including staff training and development plus the creation and implementation of sales and marketing programs.
- Performed extensive work cultivating referrals from accounts as well as from physicians and lawyers throughout the community.
- Performed market and competitive analysis.
- Performed community education through creating and conducting seminars on psychiatric illness.
- Gave marketing presentations on television.
- Designed, wrote, and produced brochures and manuals for client and family resources.
- Performed marketing activities on AIDS education as well as fund-raising for AIDS survivors.

Staff Training/Development

- Recruited, hired, and trained paraprofessionals to work with patients, plus developed recruitment and internship programs to attract physical, occupational, and speech therapists.
- Spoke at area schools and universities to develop job applicants.
- Recruited, trained, and supervised over 150 volunteers who provided medical, legal, housing, and counseling services for HIV and AIDS survivors and their families.
- Created, taught, and coordinated AIDS education courses for physician interns.

Program Development/Management

- Oversaw a $100,000 budget and a 10-person interdisciplinary team responsible for delivering vocational-rehabilitative, community reentry, and medical-management services to psychiatric, head-injured, and developmentally disabled patients.
- Performed program development for individuals with head-injured, neurological disorders. Designed a life-skills curriculum, a social-skills curriculum, and cognitive and community reentry programs.

Roy N. Givens
Page 2

- Created and conducted education courses in first aid, CPR, AIDS education, crisis prevention and intervention, CARF and HRS regulations, personnel/employee management, time management, workers' compensation issues/risk management, and organizational policies and procedures.

- Created and instituted 6-week modules for rehabilitation activities, and designed and taught community reentry and ADL classes on an individual and group basis.

- Performed case management for over 40 people with AIDS/HIV infection.

- Designed, developed, and negotiated the use of the first AIDS education curriculum at a local prison.

- Developed curricula for individual and group activities, including motor coordination, expression therapies, and arts and crafts.

EDUCATION

B.S., Education, New York University. 1985.

EMPLOYMENT HISTORY

Comprehensive Health Services, Inc., Sarasota, FL. 1995–present.
Naples Outpatient Rehabilitation Center, Naples, FL. 1994.
New Medico Rehabilitation of Florida, Wachula, FL. 1992–1994.
Hutchings Psychiatric Center/Parkside Psychosocial Center, Syracuse, NY. 1992.
Research Foundation of the State University of New York, Syracuse, NY. 1989–1991.
Kramer Psychiatric Center, Albany, NY. 1986–1989.

References furnished on request.

NUMBER SEVEN: BEING UNEMPLOYED

The 1990s have seen a tidal wave of downsizings and reorganizations sweeping across corporate America. *National Business Employment Weekly* reports that from 1991–1993 alone, over 9,000,000 people, or seven percent of the work force, found themselves out of work. One day someone was a valued member of an organization; the next, the individual was let go because of a decision made at the highest echelon in the company. The dismissal seldom had anything to do with the worker's performance. It was a corporate decision, not an individual one.

As a result, being out of work just doesn't carry the stigma it used to. When interviewers receive résumés from unemployed job hunters today, they no longer look at the person's background with skepticism and wonder what they did that was wrong, causing the company to terminate them.

Nevertheless, it's still advantageous to be employed when looking for a job. Even in the face of these widespread layoffs and early retirements, many people believe that an organization will always find a place in its ranks for a top-notch producer.

Because both the chronological and functional résumés contain dates of employment, they are dead giveaways as to whether or not someone is out of work. The disadvantage of the chronological format, however, is that it begins by announcing this fact—and some employers will immediately discard the document because they prefer to hire people who are currently employed.

A further disadvantage of the chronological format is that the person's most important work may not always have occurred at the last job. Impressive accomplishments may have been made earlier in someone's career and not get read at all. Had these accomplishments taken place in the most recent position, there's the possibility that some employers would overlook the fact that the job hunter is unemployed and bring him in for an interview.

Here's Theodore Bradisch's chronological résumé, which illustrates these two points. Theodore is out of work, and he was with his last employer for such a short period of time that he wasn't able to do anything that was particularly noteworthy.

Theodore Bradisch
409 West Shade Drive
Parrish, FL 34219
(813) 776-5410

OBJECTIVE   Artistic Director or Managing Director of a Performing-Arts Complex.

EXPERIENCE   **BRADENTON THEATER PLAYERS**, Bradenton, FL. 1994–1995.
Director of this community theater.

- Oversaw renovations of this 1923 Vaudeville Theater with 1,100 seats.

LITTLE PINEAPPLE THEATER, Sarasota, FL. 1991-1994.
Managing Director of this 45-year-old community theater.

- Administered a production budget of over $250,000 and a staff of 35 professionals and volunteers.

- Directed all marketing, membership development, administrative, accounting, personnel, and physical-plant operations.

- Wrote and managed grants for general operations and special projects.

- Coordinated 31 committees under the guidance of a 15-member board of directors.

- Developed and supervised new programs in youth education and adult workshops.

SOUTHEASTERN LOUISIANA UNIVERSITY, Hammond, LA. 1977–1991.
Instructor of Developmental Education—1989–1991.

- Created a new program for entry-level students and taught the program, consisting of study skills, critical thinking, testing skills, vocabulary, and time management.

Assistant Professor of Theater—1977–1989.

- Instructed in the production area of theater.

- Supervised the production of over 80 serious dramas, operas, musicals, dance dramas, ballets, and concerts. Responsibilities included directing, scenic design, technical direction, stage management, as well as developing and administering budgets, purchasing, inventory control, equipment maintenance, and the hiring and training of personnel.

- Directed both mainstage theater and tour productions.

- Authored *Valentino,* a dance drama chronicling Rudolph Valentino's life. Work was produced in 1983.

- Authored *A Study Guide*, published by Hunter Publications, 1980. The guide was a study tool for *Imitation: Art of the Theater*, a book surveying the history of theater in Western civilization from Greece to modern America.
- Directed a production of *Rashomon* and won the "1982 Amoco Artistic Excellence Award" and the "Director's Choice of the 1982 Louisiana Theater Arts Festival" award for best show and direction in the festival.

SOUTHERN UNIVERSITY, Baton Rouge, LA. 1974–1977.
Instructor of Theater and Speech.

- Taught Technical Theater and Public Speaking.
- Designed *Porgy and Bess* for the Louisiana Bicentennial Celebration (1976).
- Designed *Madam Butterfly* for a repertory company. Production was hailed by *Denver Post* as "An exceptional artistic solution to a difficult design problem—most marketable."
- Wrote a stage adaptation of James Thurber's *Thirteen Clocks,* by permission of The Thurber Estate. The production toured the western states for youth audiences in 1976.

EDUCATION   M.F.A., University of New Orleans, 1979.
Concentration in Theater Production, Design, and Management.

M.A., Theater Arts/Design, University of Northern Colorado, 1974.

B.A., Theater Arts, University of Northern Colorado, 1973.

References furnished on request.

Here's Theodore's functional résumé. It doesn't begin by stating that he's unemployed. Instead, it immediately conveys his most important strengths and accomplishments in the theater, both as a business manager and as an artistic director.

An employer now has every reason to read Theodore's résumé in its entirety. And when he does learn that Theodore is currently out of work, he may decide to interview him anyway, due to the strength of his qualifications. The fact that Theodore is unemployed has been minimized.

Theodore Bradisch
409 West Shade Drive
Parrish, FL 34219
(813) 776-5410

OBJECTIVE

Artistic Director or Managing Director of a Performing-Arts Complex.

THEATER-MANAGEMENT BACKGROUND

- Administered a production budget of over $250,000 and a staff of 35 professionals and volunteers.
- Directed all marketing, membership development, administrative, accounting, personnel, and physical-plant operations.
- Wrote and managed grants for general operations and special projects.
- Coordinated up to 31 committees under guidance of a 15-member board of directors.
- Developed and supervised new programs in youth education and adult workshops.
- Renovated an 1,100-seat Vaudeville theater and converted it into a modern community facility.

ARTISTIC-DIRECTION BACKGROUND

- Supervised the production of over 80 serious dramas, operas, musicals, dance dramas, ballets, and concerts.
- Performed the directing, scenic design, technical direction, and stage management.
- Directed both mainstage theater and tour productions.
- Directed a production of *Rashomon* and won the "1982 Amoco Artistic Excellence Award" and the "Director's Choice of the 1982 Louisiana Theater Arts Festival" award for best show and direction in the festival.
- Designed *Porgy and Bess* for the Louisiana Bicentennial Celebration.
- Designed *Madam Butterfly* for a repertory company. Production was hailed by *Denver Post* as "An exceptional artistic solution to a difficult design problem—most marketable."
- Wrote a stage adaptation of James Thurber's *Thirteen Clocks*, by permission of The Thurber Estate. The production toured the western states for youth audiences in 1976.

Theodore Bradisch
Page 2

EDUCATION

M.F.A., University of New Orleans, 1979.
Concentration in Theater Production, Design, and Management.

M.A., Theater Arts/Design, University of Northern Colorado, 1974.

B.A., Theater Arts, University of Northern Colorado, 1973.

References furnished on request.

A tactic that some job hunters use to conceal the fact that they're out of work is to prepare a résumé that states that they're currently employed.

Their rationale and explanation when being interviewed is that they wrote the résumé while they were still on the job and just haven't gotten around to revising it yet.

What is key here is the amount of time that's transpired since the job hunter left his company. If it's been only a week or two, that's one matter. It can easily take that amount of time to revise a résumé and have it printed.

But if someone has been unemployed for a longer period of time, then they seriously risk being accused—and rightly so—of misrepresentation.

Be careful about how long you've been out of work if your résumé states that you're currently employed.

NUMBER EIGHT: NEARING RETIREMENT AGE

It's becoming increasingly difficult for job hunters in their late forties and fifties to get the interviews they want.

The emphasis in this country is clearly on youth, and individuals who are seasoned in their career are suffering as a result.

Two myths abound. One is that senior people lack the energy and motivation of their younger counterparts. The other is that experienced workers are set in their ways and cannot adjust to a different method of doing things or a new corporate environment. Many people believe they're difficult to train.

Again, because both the chronological and functional résumés contain dates of employment, they'll reveal someone's age. When it comes to this problem area, the functional approach doesn't provide an advantage over the chronological résumé. In both documents, a job hunter's age becomes apparent at the same time—at the end of the document, when the person's first job or educational background is given.

The chronological and functional résumés of Steven Jaworsky, a 62-year-old job hunter, illustrate this point.

Steven B. Jaworsky
15 Island Drive
Palm Beach, FL 33480
(407) 582-8976

OBJECTIVE   A challenging Operations/Marketing position with P&L responsibility.

EXPERIENCE   ATLANTIC PUBLISHING, INC., Palm Beach, FL and Santa Barbara, CA.
1988–present.

General Manager, responsible for 2 magazine-publishing companies.

- Direct all operations of this $2,200,000 business, including developing and instituting management systems and controls that improved operating efficiencies and product quality.
- Manage the sales, administrative, editorial, and production departments, including a staff of 25.
- Reorganized a newly acquired magazine and turned a $120,000 annual loss into a $100,000 annual profit in less than 1 year's time.
- Decreased operating expenses 20%.
- Developed a brochure-publishing division and a resort magazine that were profitable from their inceptions. Also created a book-publishing division that operated profitably within 6 months.
- Created and instituted a subscription promotion that doubled renewal rates and increased new subscription orders by 50%.
- Designed marketing programs for direct-mail campaigns that increased paid circulation 50%.
- Set up multichannel distribution of published materials at retail, wholesale, and through mail order. Implemented a 24-hour order service for specific promotions.

PROFIT CONCEPTS, INC., DeKalb, IL. 1984–1988.

Founder and **Managing Partner** of this advertising/marketing firm that created promotions for Apple Computer, Inc. as well as for magazine publishers, retailers, and travel agencies in the Chicago, Minneapolis, and Wisconsin markets.

- Developed multimedia and direct-mail promotional campaigns that resulted in sales increases as high as 50% in 6 months.
- Analyzed clients' businesses and recommended sales, marketing, and operational changes that dramatically increased revenues, profits, and operating efficiencies.
- Created successful marketing programs for retailers: event promotion, TV, radio, direct mail, catalog, newsletter, and telemarketing.

Steven B. Jaworsky
Page 2

COMPUTER TREE, INC. and APPLETREE STEREO, INC., DeKalb, IL. 1969–1988.

Founder and **President** of a chain of computer and audio-equipment stores located throughout the state of Illinois.

* Grew sales of a 2-unit, computer-products retailer from a zero base to $1,500,000 in less than 3 years' time.

* Built a $2,000 investment in an audio-equipment store into an 8-unit chain with annual revenues of $5,000,000.

* Offered prepackaged computer systems for specific business needs, plus custom-configured systems to satisfy individual requirements.

* Hired, trained, and directed a staff of 47, including 30 inside and outside sales reps in 10 different locations.

* Implemented a product strategy to improve gross margins, increasing pretax profits by $100,000.

* Youngest person ever to be elected President of NARDA, Inc., the largest trade association in the country for consumer-electronics dealers.

* Recipient of national award, "Distinguished Dealer Award for Consumer Electronics," for having achieved the highest level of customer satisfaction.

ZENITH RADIO, INC., Chicago, IL. 1965–1969.

Sales Representative.

* Sold radios and television sets to retailers throughout the state of Illinois.

AMPEX CORPORATION, Chicago, IL. 1955–1965.

Sales Representative.

* Sold tape recorders to retailers throughout Illinois, Indiana, and Ohio.

EDUCATION   B.S., Business Administration, University of Illinois. 1955.

References furnished on request.

Steven B. Jaworsky
15 Island Drive
Palm Beach, FL 33480
(407) 582-8976

OBJECTIVE

A challenging Operations/Marketing position with P&L responsibility.

COMPUTER/CONSUMER-ELECTRONICS BACKGROUND

- Founded and managed a chain of computer and audio-equipment stores located throughout the state of Illinois.

- Grew sales of a 2-unit, computer-products retailer from a zero base to $1,500,000 in less than 3 years' time.

- Built a $2,000 investment in an audio-equipment store into an 8-unit chain with annual revenues of $5,000,000.

- Offered prepackaged computer systems for specific business needs, plus custom-configured systems to satisfy individual requirements.

- Hired, trained, and directed a staff of 47, including 30 inside and outside sales reps in 10 different locations.

- Implemented a product strategy to improve gross margins, increasing pretax profits by $100,000.

- Youngest person ever to be elected President of NARDA, Inc., the largest trade association in the country for consumer-electronics dealers.

- Recipient of national award, "Distinguished Dealer Award for Consumer Electronics," for having achieved the highest level of customer satisfaction.

PUBLISHING BACKGROUND

- As General Manager, held responsibility for 2 magazine-publishing companies located in Florida and California.

- Directed all operations of a $2,200,000 business, including developing and instituting management systems and controls that improved operating efficiencies and product quality.

- Reorganized a newly acquired magazine and turned a $120,000 annual loss into a $100,000 annual profit in less than 1 year's time.

- Decreased operating expenses 20%.

Steven B. Jaworsky
Page 2

- Managed the sales, administrative, editorial, and production departments, including a staff of 25.

- Developed a brochure-publishing division and a resort magazine that were profitable from their inception. Also created a book-publishing division that operated profitably within 6 months.

- Created and instituted a subscription promotion that doubled renewal rates and increased new subscription orders by 50%.

- Designed marketing programs for direct-mail campaigns that increased paid circulation 50%.

- Set up multichannel distribution of published materials at retail, wholesale, and through mail order. Implemented a 24-hour order service for specific promotions.

MARKETING/ADVERTISING BACKGROUND

- Established and ran an advertising/marketing firm that created promotions for Apple Computer, Inc. as well as for magazine publishers, retailers, and travel agencies in the Chicago, Minneapolis, and Wisconsin markets.

- Developed multimedia and direct-mail promotional campaigns that resulted in sales increases as high as 50% in 6 months.

- Analyzed clients' businesses and recommended sales, marketing, and operational changes that dramatically increased revenues, profits, and operating efficiencies.

- Created successful marketing programs for retailers: event promotion, TV, radio, direct mail, catalog, newsletter, and telemarketing.

EMPLOYMENT HISTORY

Atlantic Publishing, Inc., Palm Beach, FL. 1988–present.
Profit Concepts, Inc, DeKalb, IL. 1984–1988.
Computer Tree, Inc. and Appletree Stereo, Inc., DeKalb, IL. 1969–1988.
Zenith Radio, Inc., Chicago, IL. 1965–1969.
Ampex Corporation, Chicago, IL. 1955–1965.

EDUCATION

B.S., Business Administration, University of Illinois. 1955.

References furnished on request.

Since one's age is apparent, what some job hunters try to do to make themselves appear younger is to omit one or two of their jobs from their résumé. They also delete the dates from the "Education" section.

For example, Steven Jaworsky could have deleted all information concerning Ampex Corporation, leading employers to believe that his first job began with Zenith Radio in 1965. This would have made him appear to be approximately 52 years old instead of 62. And Steven could have also listed his education as follows, omitting the date, so as not to give away his true age:

Education   B.S., Business Administration, University of Illinois.

This approach to résumé writing is blatantly dishonest and will only cause embarrassment when it's discovered at the interview. Furthermore, whenever dates don't appear in the "Education" section, employers know that the job hunter is trying to hide his age. What's particularly risky about this is that an employer could assume that someone is much older than he really is.

The best way to conceal your age is to use a variation of a résumé that's often referred to as the "résumé-letter." As mentioned earlier, this approach is discussed in Chapter Seven.

You've just seen how the functional format will eliminate or minimize seven out of the eight problem areas that many job hunters encounter. There are two other things it can do that you should be aware of.

First, if you have a diverse background and are qualified to handle a number of different jobs, the functional format can be used to highlight a specific part of your background to demonstrate your qualifications for one of those positions.

As an example, let's look at the background of Joan Brady. Joan has in-depth experience in restaurant management, office-records management, and office administration. After moving to Sarasota and holding two different positions in office administration, Joan decided that she wanted to return to either restaurant management or office-records management.

First you'll see Joan's chronological résumé so you'll have a complete understanding of her background. (Notice how Joan's last two positions have nothing to do with either job that appears in her objective.) Then you'll see Joan's functional résumés, first for restaurant management, then for office-records management.

Joan C. Brady
9824 Swift St.
Sarasota, FL 34233
(813) 365-8306

OBJECTIVE   A challenging position in Restaurant Management or Office-Records Management.

EXPERIENCE   **SARASOTA TAPE COMPANY**, Sarasota, FL. 1995–1996.

Office Manager for this distributor of industrial pressure-sensitive tapes.

- Complete responsibility for performing accounts payable, accounts receivable, order entry/processing, customer service, records maintenance, collection of delinquent invoices, preparation of documents for month-end financial statements, plus light bookkeeping and correspondence.
- Received orders from customers, processed orders, and shipped products from warehouse. Directed suppliers to drop-ship as necessary.
- Performed inventory control and replenished stock.
- Searched for and located vendors to fill special orders.

ADVANCED ELECTRO-TECHNICAL SERVICES, INC., Sarasota, FL. 1994–1995.

Administrative Assistant at this electrical contracting/engineering company.

- Performed accounts payable and receivable, data entry, and payroll.
- Handled bank deposits and employee insurance, plus purchased office supplies.
- Trouble-shot customer problems and referred to appropriate technical personnel.
- Composed correspondence and maintained files.

CROWN RESTAURANT, Boston, MA. 1992–1994.

General Manager of this 200-seat restaurant open 24 hours a day.

- Planned and opened the facility. Designed the interior and purchased the equipment, furniture, furnishings, and supplies.
- Hired, trained, and managed 95 employees comprising the wait, bus, and office staff.
- Wrote the job descriptions and operating manuals.
- Researched and purchased an integrated restaurant computer system and trained wait staff in its use. Maintained continuous contact with software vendor to resolve problems and facilitate changes in menu and pricing.
- Appointed and managed shift supervisors once operations were running smoothly.
- Worked closely with vendors and handled the payroll, accounting, plus daily and monthly records.

Joan C. Brady
Page 2

ARNOLD'S, New Haven, CT. 1986–1992.

Manager of this 100-seat, casual/creative dining restaurant.

- Hired, trained, scheduled, and supervised the wait and bus staff.
- Created and implemented staff-training programs to provide the highest level in customer service and satisfaction.
- Developed marketing programs and promotional materials in conjunction with advertising agency.
- Managed inventory and performed purchasing of food, beverages, and supplies.
- Initially joined restaurant as Assistant to Owner.

LEGAL MANAGEMENT ASSISTANCE, Old Lyme, CT. 1976–1986.

Manager of this firm that provided moving and records-management services.

- Planned and directed corporate moves plus improved filing systems for large banks and law firms utilizing up to 5,000 files. Key accounts included Connecticut Bank & Trust, Bank of New England, and Fleet Bank.
- Updated and enhanced existing filing systems and also installed new state-of-the-art systems.
- Evaluated clients' filing requirements, recommended best systems to use, plus recommended appropriate computer systems for backup.
- Set up and organized new or existing file rooms and provided continuous support as needed.
- Boxed, numbered, and computerized all files prior to corporate move.
- Diagrammed all new offices and specified locations for fixtures, furniture, and equipment.
- Scheduled, coordinated, and monitored activities of moving company.
- Sold old furniture and purchased new furniture as required.

HARTFORD SAVINGS & LOAN ASSOCIATION, Hartford, CT. 1972–1976.

Administrative Assistant to the President and Chairman of the Board.

- Assisted in planning, coordinating, and supervising this saving and loan's move from one location to another.
- Set up all board of directors and committee meetings including taking and preparing minutes.
- Coordinated numerous activities of senior management and board members.
- Researched, recommended, and processed requests for charitable contributions.

EDUCATION   B.S., Business Administration, Boston University, 1972.

References furnished on request.

Joan C. Brady
9824 Swift Road
Sarasota, FL 34233
(813) 365-8306

OBJECTIVE

A challenging position in Restaurant Management.

RESTAURANT-MANAGEMENT EXPERIENCE

- Background includes opening a new restaurant plus assuming management responsibilities at an existing location. Facilities included casual/creative dining and travelers' restaurants.

- Planned and opened a 200-seat restaurant that operated 24 hours a day. Designed the facility plus purchased the equipment, furniture, furnishings, and supplies.

- Hired, trained, and managed up to 95 employees comprising the wait, bus, and office staff.

- Wrote job descriptions and operating manuals.

- Created and implemented staff-training programs to provide the highest level in customer service and satisfaction.

- Developed marketing programs and promotional materials in conjunction with advertising agency.

- Researched and purchased an integrated restaurant computer system and trained wait staff in its use. Maintained continuous contact with software vendor to resolve problems and facilitate changes in menu and pricing.

- Appointed, trained, and managed shift supervisors.

- Managed inventory control and performed purchasing of food, beverages, and supplies.

- Handled payroll, accounting, plus daily and monthly records.

OFFICE-ADMINISTRATION EXPERIENCE

- Managed financial and administrative functions of business offices.

- Interfaced extensively with customers and vendors.

- Assisted senior management and board of directors at a savings and loan, including coordinating their activities plus taking and preparing minutes.

Joan C. Brady
Page 2

EDUCATION

B.S., Business Administration, Boston University, 1972.

EMPLOYMENT HISTORY

Sarasota Tape Company, Sarasota, FL. 1995–1996.
Advanced Electro-Technical Services, Inc., Sarasota, FL. 1994–1995.
Crown Restaurant, Boston, MA. 1992–1994.
Arnold's, New Haven, CT. 1986–1992.
Legal Management Assistance, Old Lyme, CT. 1976–1986.
Hartford Savings & Loan Association, Hartford, CT. 1972–1976.

References furnished on request.

Joan C. Brady
9824 Swift St.
Sarasota, FL 34233
(813) 365-8306

OBJECTIVE

A challenging position with a growing company in the Records-Management business.

RECORDS-MANAGEMENT BACKGROUND

- 10 years' experience in the records-management business.
- Planned and directed corporate moves plus improved filing systems for large banks and law firms utilizing up to 5,000 files. Key accounts included Connecticut Bank & Trust, Bank of New England, and Fleet Bank.
- Updated and enhanced existing filing systems and also installed new state-of-the-art systems.
- Evaluated clients' filing requirements, recommended best systems to use, plus recommended appropriate computer systems for backup.
- Set up and organized new or existing file rooms and provided continuous support as needed.
- Boxed, numbered, and computerized all files prior to corporate move.
- Diagrammed all new offices and specified locations for fixtures, furniture, and equipment.
- Scheduled, coordinated, and monitored activities of moving company.
- Sold old furniture and purchased new furniture as required.

RESTAURANT-MANAGEMENT/ADMINISTRATIVE EXPERIENCE

- Opened and managed restaurants seating up to 200 diners and employing up to 95 people.
- Complete responsibility for hiring, training, and supervising all personnel for the business office and front-of-the-house operations.
- Assisted senior management and board of directors at a savings and loan, including coordinating their activities plus taking and preparing minutes.

EDUCATION

B.S., Business Administration, Boston University, 1972.

Joan C. Brady
Page 2

EMPLOYMENT HISTORY

Sarasota Tape Company, Sarasota, FL. 1995–1996.
Advanced Electro-Technical Services, Inc., Sarasota, FL. 1994–1995.
Crown Restaurant, Boston, MA. 1992–1994.
Arnold's, New Haven, CT. 1986–1992.
Legal Management Assistance, Old Lyme, CT. 1976–1986.
Hartford Savings & Loan Association, Hartford, CT. 1972–1976.

References furnished on request.

There's one more functional résumé to discuss, and it's called the "Accomplishments" or "Career History" résumé. This document lists an individual's responsibilities and achievements in one particular kind of work instead of describing duties and accomplishments from all the different jobs that he has performed.

This résumé is often used by job hunters whose career has consisted of doing the same type of work for a number of different companies. It enables them to avoid a great deal of repetition.

Here's an example of this résumé, utilizing the background of a job hunter who has been in the business of paving roadways his entire life:

Gary Maddox
607 Brown Ave.
Nokomis, FL 34275
(813) 484-9798

PROFILE

Over 20 years' experience constructing roadways. Customers have included municipalities plus private corporations such as U.S. Homes and Walt Disney. Possess outstanding planning, organizational, and communication skills. An excellent leader and motivator of field personnel.

CAREER SUMMARY

- Complete project responsibility from initial planning stage to completion. Projects consisted of rough grading, fine grading, concrete, plus paving of streets, parking lots, subdivisions, and private roads.

- Estimated jobs and prepared bids and proposals, both as prime and subcontractor. Also performed job costing.

- Continuously met with prospective customers to generate new business—secured contracts from $100,000 to over $7,000,000.

- Worked with city and county agencies to get plans approved and projects accepted.

- Scheduled projects, obtained quotes from subcontractors, and let subcontracts ranging from $30,000 to $1,000,000.

- Purchased light and heavy equipment and materials.

- Set construction schedules and supervised all work. Directed crews of up to 60 laborers, 5 foremen, and 1 superintendent. Also oversaw all subcontract work, including utilities, storm drain, sewer, and electrical.

- Coordinated construction activities with architects, engineers, and inspectors.

- Monitored work-in-process to ensure adherence to specifications and schedules. Resolved plans/specs disputes.

- Met with bankers to arrange short-term financing as needed.

- Managed office administration including schedules, systems and procedures, payables, receivables, bookkeeping, and final payment collection. Met with attorneys to set up collection procedures when necessary.

Gary Maddox
Page 2

EDUCATION

Certificate, All American Contracting School, Pomona, CA. 1980.

A.A., Business Management, Santa Ana College, Santa Ana, CA. 1971.

EMPLOYMENT HISTORY

Baird-Frey, Inc., Apple Valley, CA. 1988–1995. Project Manager/Chief Estimator.
Olah Equipment Company, Inc., Upland, CA. 1987–1988. Co-Owner.
Summit Grading and Paving, Corona, CA. 1983–1987. Chief Estimator.
All American Asphalt, Corona, CA. 1982. Chief Estimator.
Barrett Construction Company, Inc., Upland, CA. 1980–1982. Estimator.
All American Asphalt, Corona, CA. 1979–1980. Estimator.
Sully-Miller Contracting, Orange, CA. 1978–1979. Estimator.
R.J. Noble Company, Orange, CA. 1972–1978. Estimator/Foreman.

References furnished on request.

DRAWBACKS TO THE FUNCTIONAL FORMAT

While its's clear that the functional format gives you enormous flexibility in discussing your work experience and also enables you to highlight your strengths while eliminating or at least offsetting key problem areas, this type of résumé, like the chronological, has its drawbacks.

First of all, some employers don't like reading functional résumés because it's difficult to tell with which companies accomplishments and duties occurred.

Second, some employers know that one of the purposes of this format can be to conceal liabilities (They may have used it themselves for this very reason!), so they can be suspicious when they receive a functional résumé.

In order to decide which approach will be the best for your individual situation, you need to weigh the severity of the problem areas you're trying to overcome against the strength of your qualifications. As a general rule, the more serious your liabilities, the more you'll need to use the functional approach; however, the stronger your qualifications, the more your attributes will tend to offset these problem areas.

While it's a judgment call as to the best way to proceed, the likelihood is that the functional résumé will produce many more interviews.

When using a functional résumé, there are also certain questions you can expect to be asked when being interviewed.

The question you'll hear the most is "Which of your different activities pertain to which employers?" Begin your response by discussing that part of your work experience that's the most relevant to the job you're being interviewed for. Then tell the interviewer about your other activities and with which employers they occurred.

Another question you can expect to hear will be along the lines of: "Why did you describe your background this way instead of listing your duties by employer?" Explain that what you want to emphasize about yourself is your experience and capability in certain areas, not the companies you've worked for and when you were with them.

At a certain point in the interview, the very problem areas that your résumé successfully overcame will inevitably surface, and you must be ready to discuss these matters.

Don't feel like you're being put on the defensive, however, when going over these aspects of your background. Remember, the interviewer is impressed with your experience and that's why your having a face-to-face meeting with him at this time. Just be sure you have good explanations prepared for why you left your employers, why you joined certain organizations, and why it took the amount of time that it did. If you find that you're discussing a point that's embarrassing—such as the fact that you were terminated by an employer or held a position of decreased responsibility—explain why the situation occurred, what you learned from it, and why, today, you're stronger both professionally and personally as a result. Turn the negative into a positive.

CHAPTER 3

THE SECONDARY SECTIONS

The sections that have been discussed so far—objective, profile, education, and work experience—are the crux of the résumé for most job hunters and usually carry the key information that employers look for.

The secondary sections, however, can sometimes be helpful for furthering a job hunter's qualifications. For example, they can be used to provide additional information that shows that someone has certain skills, training, or accomplishments that are important in his line of work. They can demonstrate that the individual gets along well with others and is effective in a group setting. They can also be used to provide information about personal characteristics that will make the person successful in his field.

PROFESSIONAL ORGANIZATIONS

If you belong to professional organizations, always include this information. It will demonstrate a sincere interest in your work. When someone has no involvement with their career outside of regular business hours, they can't be expected to have any deep commitment to it.

If you happen to be (or have been in the past) an officer of an organization, this will be especially impressive. It will convey leadership qualities as well as the fact that you're held in high esteem by your colleagues.

Here's an example of this section from a résumé of a social worker whose specialty is gerontology:

PROFESSIONAL   National Association of Private Geriatric Care
ORGANIZATIONS   Managers.

Sigma Phi Omega-National Academic and
Professional Society in Gerontology.

Gerontological Society of America.

Southern Gerontological Society.

Gerontological Society of Florida.

Secretary, Sarasota County Aging Network.
Member of the Steering Committee.

Member of the Publicity Committee.

You can also use memberships in organizations other than professional ones to convey personal information about yourself when you feel it will be advantageous to do so. Job hunters sometimes use this section to communicate their religion, race, ethnic background, sexual orientation, or the fact that they are physically challenged.

As an example, a black job hunter saw so many ads that stated "Minorities are encouraged to apply" that he prepared a special résumé offering this information in a section titled "Organizations."

ORGANIZATIONS   African-American Alliance.

Center for Black Studies.

And here's how a gay male, who was interested only in companies that had a large gay population, used this section to communicate his sexual preference:

MEMBERSHIPS   Sarasota Gay Alliance.

Referral Counselor, Manasota AIDS Support.

Area Contact Person, Parents and Friends of Lesbians and Gays.

Other names you can use for this section are "Affiliations" and "Memberships."

COMMUNITY ACTIVITIES

Participation in community activities can also be used to enhance your qualifications. Just like memberships in professional organizations, they, too, will convey your enthusiasm for your field.

Following is what the wellness coordinator for a hospital stated in this section:

COMMUNITY ACTIVITIES	Planned Approach to Community Health, Sarasota County, Florida.
	The Health Advisory Council, Sarasota, Florida.
	The Coalition on Child Abuse, Sarasota, Florida.
	The School Advisory Council, Sarasota County, Florida.
	Steering Committee on Women's Issues, Big Brothers/Big Sisters.

Another name for this section is "Volunteer Positions."

Listing community activities can also be used to broaden your background and show that you're an interesting and well-rounded person who enjoys working with others and is a joiner versus a loner. Such traits can be especially important for positions that require a highly social individual with an outgoing personality. You can even include memberships in clubs in this section. Here's an example:

COMMUNITY ACTIVITIES/ CLUBS	Toastmasters International.
	Sarasota County Special Olympics.
	The Jazz Club of Sarasota.
	Little League Baseball Coach.
	Big Brothers/Big Sisters of Sarasota.
	Sarasota Rugby Club.

HONORS AND AWARDS

If you've received honors or awards for having performed outstanding work on the job, this should always appear in your résumé. There's no better testimonial to your expertise.

A dental assistant put down:

HONORS AND AWARDS	Recipient of the first award for "Outstanding Service" ever given by the American Red Cross at my military installation.
	"Red Cross Volunteer of the Quarter, October–December, 1987.

LICENSES AND CERTIFICATIONS

In some professions, receiving licensure or certification is a prerequisite for employment in the field. This information should always appear in your résumé.

Here's what a job hunter whose background consists of managing condominiums and mobile-home complexes wrote:

LICENSES   State of Florida Community Association Manager. 1994. #14749.

State of Florida Real Estate Broker. 1982. #BK 0205132.

And here's what a real-estate appraiser put down:

CERTIFICATIONS   Florida Certified General Real Estate Appraiser. 1993. #RZ 0001790.

"Certified Florida Evaluator," Florida Department of Revenue. 1988.

PATENTS

Along with having received honors and awards at work, holding a patent is extremely impressive.

Following is the patent information for an inventor of a product used to alleviate skin irritation:

PATENT   "Method For Alleviating Skin Irritation By Formulations Containing Superoxide Dismutase." Patent Number; 4,695,456. September 22, 1987.

PUBLICATIONS

If you've had a book published or have written an article that was published by a magazine or newspaper, this is something to be proud of and to include in your résumé, especially if the material was work-related.

The chief financial officer for a museum treated this section as follows:

PUBLICATION   Coauthor, *Fundamentals of Financial Management Study Guide*, Fourth Edition, CBS Publishing. 1985.

And here's what a real-estate broker wrote:

PUBLICATION   "What Is the Business Worth?" *Real Estate Today*.
                    May, 1979.

In order to use this section, you need not have written a full-length book or have been published by a nationally recognized magazine. If you wrote something for your employer's house organ or for an organization's newsletter, for example, employers will want to know about this.

Following is how a massage therapist made use of this section with an article he wrote that appeared in his church's newsletter:

PUBLICATION   "Reducing Anxiety and Stress through Massage
                    Therapy," *Mind and Heart*, May, 1993.

FOREIGN LANGUAGES

In some jobs, fluency in or familiarization with one or more foreign languages is a plus and should appear in a résumé.

Here's what one job hunter wrote, who wanted to be an airline hostess for an international airline.

FOREIGN   Fluent in French, Flemish, and Italian. Able
LANGUAGES   to read Spanish and Portuguese.

COMPUTER SKILLS

Proficiency with computers is becoming increasingly important in a wide range of positions and occupations. If you're computer literate and use computers in your work, be sure to include this information.

An executive secretary/administrative assistant wrote:

COMPUTER SKILLS WordPerfect 5.1.

                    Microsoft Word 6.0.

                    Excel.

                    Lotus 1.2.3.

                    Pagemaker.

PART-TIME JOBS AND COLLEGE WORK EXPERIENCE

These employment experiences will be of use only to two types of job hunters: the person who is pursuing a career change and the recent college graduate. How to discuss these kinds of positions is explained in Chapter Five.

HOBBIES AND INTERESTS

A decade or two ago, it was common practice for job hunters to state in their résumé what their hobbies and interests were. The thinking was that this gave potential employers information about the personal side of the applicant.

Today, with so many government restrictions on the types of questions interviewers are allowed to ask job applicants, this kind of information seldom appears. Just as the interview is focusing increasingly on work-related issues, the résumé is becoming less of a personal document.

If you do have hobbies or interests, however, that directly relate to your field and you believe that mentioning them in your résumé will add to your credibility, then by all means list them. Here's what a young electrical design engineer who wanted to join a stereo-equipment manufacturer wrote:

HOBBIES   Design and build tuners, amplifiers, and speakers.

Subscribe to *Stereophile*, *Audio Video Interiors*, and *Audio Video International*.

MILITARY EXPERIENCE

Employers aren't as interested in military experience as much as they used to be, and it's seldom elaborated on in a résumé. One of the reasons for this was our involvement in the Vietnam War. All the negative sentiment about our role in the conflict changed the way many Americans feel about armed combat, even training for it. There are two instances, however, when military experience is very important and should be discussed in depth.

The first situation is when all of, or a good part of, someone's work background and training occurred during military duty and pertains to the kind of work being sought in civilian life. This is bona fide work experience, and it should be explained in detail. The résumé of Brendan Petty illustrates this point.

Brendan G. Petty
1302 40th Street West
Bradenton, FL 34209
(813) 749-3979

OBJECTIVE   A challenging management position providing the opportunity to utilize a
leadership background plus proven ability to achieve goals and objectives
independent of supervision.

PROFILE   10 years' supervisory experience in the U.S. Army with the responsibility
for training and directing small groups of personnel. Possess excellent
planning, organizational, communication, and motivational skills.

EXPERIENCE   **COLOR WORKS**, Bradenton, FL. 1993–1995.

Owner/Operator of this company that applied protective finishes to
automobiles, boats, and aircraft.

- Set up the business and held complete responsibility for marketing,
  advertising, and daily operations.

U.S. ARMY, Ft. Sill, OK; Ft. Raleigh, KS; Ft. Carson, CO; Camp
Essayons, Korea. 1982–1993. Sergeant E-5.

Headquarters Section Chief - 1992–1993.
Crew Chief (Multiple Launch Rocket Systems) - 1987–1992.
Platoon Sergeant - 1986–1987.
Headquarters Section Chief - 1984–1986.

- Directed up to 18 personnel.

- Scheduled daily activities including classroom assignments.

- Trained personnel in Weapons and Tactics, Computer Data Entry,
  Combat Sustainment, and Equal Opportunity.

- Provided technical assistance in operating multiple-launch rocket
  systems.

- Supervised maintenance and construction activities, and assured
  compliance with safety procedures.

- Read, interpreted, and collected intelligence information.

- Evaluated performance of personnel, wrote performance reports, and
  made recommendations for promotions.

EDUCATION   Diploma, Glen Academy, Brunswick, GA. 1987.

References furnished on request.

The second instance when military background is important is when someone received a distinguished honor or award, or performed a significant leadership role. This is particularly important when the accolade was for combat and the individual will be working in a setting that requires an aggressive, forcible personality. In this instance, it isn't necessary to elaborate on the experience; just citing the commendation will suffice.

Here are two examples:

MILITARY   U.S. Army, 1964–1967. E-5. Paratrooper in Vietnam. Recipient of Purple Heart and Bronze Star with Valor.

MILITARY   United States Navy, 1962–1969. Lieutenant Commander.

PERSONAL DATA

A brief section containing personal information used to be part and parcel of a job hunter's résumé. The following was a typical entry on a résumé in the 1970s and earlier:

PERSONAL   6'2", 185 lbs. Married with two children. Excellent health. Willing to travel and relocate.

Today, the "Personal" section has all but disappeared, due to federal and state laws requiring employers to discuss only job-related matters with applicants. When personal information is used, however, height, weight, and physical condition hardly ever appear.

In the event that there's something special about you that you want potential employers to be aware of and it doesn't fit into any of the other sections of your résumé, include it here.

Here's what a job hunter in his fifties put down in order to convey to employers that he is active and energetic. His goal was to offset the fact that he was getting on in years.

PERSONAL   Enjoy racquetball, jogging, and swimming.

CHAPTER 4

PUTTING IT ALL TOGETHER

Now that you understand the different sections of the résumé and the kinds of information you can offer about yourself, you're almost ready to begin writing your first draft. First, though, you need to answer these four questions:

1. *Do I use an objective or a profile?* You might be seeking one specific position or be considering a variety of jobs; this will determine how you begin your résumé.
2. *Where do I place my educational background, at the beginning of my résumé or toward the end?* You need to decide how important your education is for the kind of work you want to do and where it should appear in your résumé.
3. *Do I use the chronological or functional format for describing my work experience?* You must take into account whether you're seeking advancement in the same field or whether you want to make a career change. Also, you need to decide whether or not you have serious liabilities in your background to overcome.
4. *Do I want to use any of the secondary sections and, if so, which ones and where should they appear?* You must decide what you want employers to know about you in addition to your work responsibilities, accomplishments, and duties. You also need to determine how important this information is and whether it should appear early in your résumé or toward the end.

Once you've considered these factors and have made these decisions, you'll know the best way to present your background and organize your résumé. You'll be ready to write your first draft.

THE FIRST DRAFT

Create a letterhead that's centered at the top of the first page. This will consist of your name, street address, town or city in which you live, state, zip code, and home telephone number. Include your fax number if you have one.

If you're currently employed, don't list your business number. You don't want prospective employers to think that you're planning on conducting your job search on company time and at company expense. (Granted, most people make and receive job-search calls from their office and you'll probably be one of them. Just don't begin communications with prospective employers by announcing that you'll be using company time for this purpose.)

Next, state your job objective if you'll be using one. Refer to the objectives that appear on pages 5–7 for guidelines in what to say about your goal. Note that key words are often capitalized.

If you'll be using a profile, don't work on this statement until after you've completed your draft. At this time, you'll know exactly what you'll be saying about yourself and what you'll want to highlight. Once you have this overview, it will be much easier to compose your profile. When you're ready to write this statement, review the profiles on pages 8 and 9 to help you decide what to say.

A powerful combination and especially effective way to begin a résumé is to state an objective that is followed by a profile. This background summary will immediately convey your ability to perform the position you're seeking.

The next section will be either your educational background, one of the secondary sections, or your work experience.

If you're planning on using a secondary section this early in your résumé, be sure the information you're offering is vital. Otherwise, it should come after your work experience. The same applies to stating your educational background at this time.

We now come to your work experience, which is usually the most important part of a résumé. When describing your different activities, you'll be using either the chronological or functional format.

Here are guidelines to follow for both approaches. While the chronological format might not be the one you plan on using, I'm going to discuss it first because it's the more complex of the two. Gary Sevitch's résumé on page 16 will serve as an example.

THE CHRONOLOGICAL FORMAT

As explained earlier, this format presents work experience in reverse chronological order.

Begin each employment situation by stating the name of your employer, the location by city and state, then dates of employment expressed in years, not months and years. Don't include an organization's street address, zip code, or telephone number.

Next, state the products or services the organization offers, as well as its size, if you feel the latter would be beneficial.

Explaining products, services, and size can be provided in two different ways. One method is to present this information in a separate sentence, as Gary Sevitch did when he discussed his Garson's experience. Another approach is to insert this information just after your title. Gary did this with his other employers. The size of an organization can be expressed by giving its sales volume or number of employees. The latter is often used with companies that are privately owned, when sales figures aren't made public.

Next, state your job title, if you haven't already done so. Also, if this position consisted of numerous responsibilities, list them, as Gary did when he was general manager at Garson's. This overview informs employers of the scope of your activities.

The most important part of your work experience now appears: your accomplishments and duties. Every prospective employer will want to know where your strengths and talents lie and what specific benefits accrued to a company as a result of your efforts. Past performance is clearly the best indicator of future performance!

There's no hard and fast rule for the number of accomplishments or duties you should list for each position. A good number to use is between two and five. If you have a large number of accomplishments, however, you might not state any duties at all (this was the case with Gary's experience at Garson's; each entry was an accomplishment). If you have only one or two accomplishments, then you might decide to include one or two duties to give breadth to your experience (Gary did this at both Decorama and Gulf Coast Home Furnishings).

The important point is to provide enough information about yourself so that potential employers will know exactly what you did and will have a clear understanding of your capability and qualifications.

When describing your accomplishments and duties, present them in the order of their importance for the kind of work you want to do. Remember, the purpose of your résumé is to convey your ability to perform this job.

When wording your accomplishments and duties, be sure your sentences are short and crisp. Long sentences lack power and can be boring to read. Also, begin each accomplishment and duty with an "action" word. Look at the résumés you've already seen and note how the sentences begin with strong verbs such as "increased," "upgraded," "revamped," "created," and "implemented." Never begin a sentence by stating, "I increased. . . ," "I upgraded. . . ," or "I revamped. . . ." etc. For your convenience, here is a list of 220 action words from which to choose:

accelerated	composed	elected
accounted for	conceived of	eliminated
achieved	conceptualized	enforced
acted	conducted	enhanced
adapted	consolidated	enlarged
addressed	constructed	enlisted
administered	consulted	established
advertised	contracted	estimated
adopted	contributed to	evaluated
advanced	controlled	examined
advised	convinced	exhibited
aligned	coordinated	expanded
analyzed	counseled	expedited
anticipated	created	experimented
arbitrated	danced	explained
appraised	debated	fabricated
approved	decided	facilitated
arranged	decorated	financed
ascertained	decreased	fixed
assembled	defined	formulated
assessed	delegated	founded
assigned	demonstrated	gathered
attained	designed	generated
audited	detected	guided
augmented	determined	handled
automated	developed	headed
budgeted	devised	hypnotized
built	diagnosed	identified
calculated	directed	illustrated
cared for	discovered	implemented
charted	displayed	improved
checked	disproved	increased
classified	diverted	influenced
collected	drafted	informed
communicated	drew	initiated
complied	edited	innovated
completed	effected	inspired

installed	prioritized	sketched
instituted	processed	sold
instructed	produced	solved
integrated	projected	sorted
interpreted	promoted	spearheaded
invented	proposed	spoke
investigated	proved	started
judged	provided	streamlined
launched	publicized	strengthened
lectured	published	structured
led	purchased	studied
maintained	questioned	summarized
managed	realigned	supervised
manufactured	recommended	supported
mediated	reconciled	surveyed
molded	recorded	synchronized
monitored	reduced	synergized
motivated	rehabilitated	synthesized
navigated	reinforced	systematized
negotiated	reorganized	tabulated
observed	repaired	taught
operated	reported	tested
ordered	researched	trained
organized	resolved	transcribed
originated	restored	translated
oversaw	restructured	transmitted
painted	revamped	triggered
participated in	reviewed	trouble-shot
perceived	revised	unified
performed	saved	united
persuaded	scheduled	upgraded
planned	separated	verbalized
predicted	served	was awarded
prepared	serviced	was promoted
prescribed	set up	won
presented	shaped	wrote

Whenever possible, use *numbers* to convey the *extent* of your accomplishments and duties. It's much more impressive to state "Increased profits 72% in 4 years" than it is to write "Significantly boosted profits." Employers will want to know *how well* you did something, not just *what* you did.

Notice that all the accomplishments and duties are preceded by bullets. These marks are extremely effective in résumé writing. They make a résumé easy to read because they guide the reader's eye to the key

points that the job hunter wants him to know about. They also accentu-
ate the statements and give them power.

Information isn't nearly as convincing when it's buried within a paragraph. For example, here's the experience section from Gary Sevitch's
résumé, only now it appears in paragraph form without any bullets. It's
not nearly as easy or as exciting to read. Compare the two.

EXPERIENCE   **GARSON'S INC.**, Sarasota, FL. 1990–present.
Company is a furniture retailer with annual sales of
$5,000,000.

General Manager with complete responsibility for P&L,
Sales, Purchasing, Merchandising, Advertising/Sales
Promotion, and Administration.

Increased profits 72% in 4 years. Upgraded and modernized
the showroom. Revamped purchasing department and
installed new vendors. Created traffic-producing advertising
and sales-promotion programs. Implemented effective
incentive programs for sales staff.

DECORAMA, Bradenton, FL. 1985–1990.

Sales Manager for this retailer of furniture and home furnishings. Annual sales: $3,000,000.

Increased sales an average of 20% per year over a 5-year
period. Recruited, hired, trained, and motivated a sales
staff of 6. Conducted training sessions on new products as
well as on effective sales and closing techniques. Created
successful print-, radio-, and television-advertising campaigns.

GULF COAST HOME FURNISHINGS, Sarasota, FL.
1978–1985.

Assistant Sales Manager at this $1,000,000 retailer of cur-
tains, draperies, and bedspreads.

#1 sales producer—consistently exceeded quota.
Interviewed potential Sales Associates and helped train new
hires. Assisted Sales Manager with merchandising, displays, and advertising/sales-promotion programs.

CONNIE'S CURTAINS, Venice, FL. 1976–1978.

Sales Associate for this retailer of curtains and draperies.

There's one final point to discuss about the way you word an accomplishment. It concerns how much information you provide. In some

instances you might want to explain *what* you did, but hold back on explaining *how* you did something. For example, let's say a résumé states,

- Increased revenues 25% the first 6 months and reduced expenses by 12%.

Now this is a great accomplishment, and the reader is immediately impressed when he sees it. Sales went up, costs went down, and all this happened in just six months' time! But what the reader doesn't know—and really wants to know—is *how* this accomplishment occurred, the specific steps that were taken to make it possible. He wonders, Did the job hunter hire more sales people? Did he replace some sales people? Did he retrain his sales force? Did he bring in new or different products or services? Did he institute new promotional programs? He also wonders, How did the job hunter reduce expenses? Did he let people go? Did he change vendors and suppliers? Did he renegotiate bank financing?

By not providing this information, the reader's curiosity is aroused. As a result, between learning about the impressive accomplishment that's been made and the allure of the unknown, the reader has all the incentive that's needed to bring the job hunter in for an interview.

On some occasions you might decide that it's advantageous to explain *how* you accomplished something. You should always do this when you utilized a technology or methodology that's in great demand, or when you believe the steps you took will be as important to a prospective employer as the accomplishment itself. It's a judgment call on your part as to which approach you think will be the most effective.

As a general rule, an accomplishment will have more impact if you state *what* you did and omit *how* you did it. This creates mystique, and in marketing circles this is known as "selling the sizzle but not the steak."

When deciding on what to say about yourself, in order to ensure that you include your most important accomplishments and duties, ask yourself these questions:

What have I done that I'm the most proud of?
What have I done that I have received a lot of praise on?
What have I done that was new or different, innovative and resourceful?
What have I done that I really want prospective employers to know about?

These are the accomplishments that you want to emphasize. The most important ones will be the things you did that were new or different along with the benefits your employer realized as a result. You might have come up with a new idea for a product or service or devised a better way of handling a certain problem or situation. If so, state this on your résumé. When preparing your first draft, it's appropriate to offer the greatest amount of information about your current or most recent position. Notice that Gary Sevitch provided increased amounts of information as his work experience became more current. Whoever hires Gary is going to do so because of his recent experience and accomplishments as a general manager. Whatever Gary did before reaching this level served only as a springboard for his successes.

When writing a chronological résumé, never include the names and titles of your current or previous managers. If an employer wants this information, he'll ask you for it.

Also, don't give your reasons for having left your employers. Some job hunters will state after discussing each company "Left company for a better opportunity" or "Left company for more money." All this does is plant the seed that you'll leave your next job as soon as you find a better position or if someone offers you a higher salary. Additionally, making a remark like "The company went out of business" or "The company declared bankruptcy" will cause prospective employers to question your vision and foresight.

You don't need to defend yourself for having left a company. At your interviews, you'll have ample opportunity to explain why you left an organization.

When using the chronological format for describing work experience, different names for this section include "Experience," "Work Experience," "Professional Experience," "Work Background," and "Professional Background."

THE FUNCTIONAL FORMAT

When composing a résumé utilizing the functional format, the key decision to make is which parts of your background you want to highlight.

You might want to emphasize what you accomplished in a certain *job*, and use a heading, or headings, such as "Sales," "Marketing," "Finance," "Accounting," "Manufacturing," "Quality Control," "Research and Development," "Administration," "Data Processing," or "Management Information Systems."

Or you might want to discuss your experience with or knowledge of a particular *type of product*, as Alexa Brookline did on page 33 under "Art-Supplies Background."

Whatever it is that you want prospective employers to know about your background, that's what you'll discuss. For examples of numerous possibilities, review the functional formats that appear in Chapter Two as well as throughout this book. You'll note that discussing two to four functional areas is the customary number.

When describing your responsibilities, duties, and accomplishments, follow the same procedures you would for writing a chronological résumé. Use short, concise sentences that begin with action words, and present information in the order of its importance for the kind of work you want to do. Always use bullets.

A difference between the functional and chronological formats is that sometimes it's not possible in the functional approach to place immediately after a heading a separate sentence that states what business an employer was in or what its size was (this is because you're grouping experiences with *several* employers under this heading). If you want prospective employers to have this kind of information, here's an example of how to provide it:

- Decreased in-house advertising production costs by 25% at a $10,000,000 dealer of stamps and coins.

By adding "at a $10,000,000 dealer of stamps and coins," this job hunter informs prospective employers of the business his company was in as well as its size.

Once you've completed the work experience section of your draft, the remaining parts of your background to discuss are the secondary sections and your educational training, if you haven't already described the latter. Present these sections in the order of their importance. Most people put their education last.

Conclude your résumé with the statement "References furnished on request." In the event that you don't have enough room on your finished résumé for this remark, omit it. It has become a formality. All employers know that they can obtain references from you if they want them.

THINGS TO AVOID

While preparing the first draft of your résumé, there are things you want to avoid regardless of whether you're using the chronological or functional format. While some are rather benign, others are land mines and turn employers off. They can cause immediate rejection.

- Stating "Résumé" or "Résumé of" above or beneath your letterhead. You don't need to describe what this document is. Everyone will know it's a résumé.

- Citing the date that your résumé was prepared. There's no reason to advertise how long you've been looking for a job, especially if it's been for an extended period of time. In the event that your résumé is hot off the press, this won't give you an advantage, either.

• Using the words "I" or "my" when stating a job objective. Many employers feel that these words sound childish when used in this statement.

For example:

OBJECTIVE I'm seeking a key-account sales position in the specialty-chemicals business, where I can apply my extensive product knowledge plus strong following with chemical purchasing agents.

What's preferable is:

OBJECTIVE Key-account sales position in the specialty-chemicals business. Seeking to utilize extensive product knowledge plus a strong following with chemical purchasing agents.

For some reason, employers don't mind the use of "I" and "my" when a job hunter is a graduating student or is in a field where he has a nurturing and supportive relationship with the people with whom he works, such as in the health-care, social services, and educational fields.

• Using cliches. For years, interviewers have been reading résumés that state how "dynamic," "success-driven," "self-motivated" or "results-oriented" someone is, or how the applicant has a "take-charge" personality or a "hands-on" management style, or that the person is "people-oriented" or is a "shirtsleeves" executive. Employers are tired of hearing these cliches. Avoid them, especially in the "Profile" section. If there are qualities you want to convey about yourself, the best way to do this is through the manner in which you describe your responsibilities and accomplishments.

• Making vague statements. Be really specific when discussing your responsibilities and duties.

If people don't know exactly what you've done, they're not going to want to interview you. For example, instead of stating,

• Performed extensive customer interface concerning shipment of merchandise.

say,

• Resolved customers' problems regarding delivery of merchandise. Contacted plant or warehouse to ascertain firm shipping dates and immediately advised customers. Traced shipments with carriers when necessary.

As another example, instead of stating,

- Coordinated special events and fund-raisers.

say,

- Located, negotiated for, and obtained sites for special events and fund-raisers.
- Hired and supervised required subcontractors, wrote and placed publicity, composed program books, and sold advertising space.

When explaining your duties, also make every effort to avoid beginning sentences with "Participated in," "Involved with," "Active in," "Contributed to," and "Played a role in." These words suggest that you didn't do anything meaningful.

Equally important, don't glorify your duties by using language where no one will understand what you did. For example, if you're a property manager or gardener, don't write, Responsible for the environmental enhancement and safety of a small Sarasota community.

The following is preferable:

- Responsible for maintaining the grounds, pool, and spa of a 32-unit retirement community.
- Continually checked the alarm systems to ensure that they were operational.

- Repeating the same words. Certain words automatically lend themselves to résumé writing, for example, *created, managed,* and *implemented.* You must watch your language to make sure that you don't overuse such words. Doing so will make your résumé boring to read.

Vary your language as much as possible, especially in the way you begin your sentences. Here, the list of action verbs on pages 92and 93 will be helpful. For example, instead of saying *created,* you can state *designed, developed, devised, formulated,* or *established.* You can replace *managed* with *directed, oversaw, administered,* and *supervised.* You can substitute *instituted, set up,* and *effected* for *implemented.* In the event that you can't think of a good alternate for a word, use a thesaurus.

- Using lengthy, run-on statements. As already discussed, your statements should be short, crisp, and to the point.

Be sure you never write anything like:

- Conducted research to identify potential customers, cold-called each prospect to introduce company and its products, set up appointments, explained features and benefits of products being offered, answered questions and overcame objections, and achieved closing ratio of 25%.

What's much more powerful is:

- Identified potential customers, cold-called to set up appointments, and closed 25% of prospects.

There's an expression in the advertising business: "Less is more." The above exemplifies this point.

- Stating your membership in an organization that indicates your race, religion, political preference, or some other personal matter that might be controversial. Don't provide this kind of information unless you're absolutely certain that it will increase your chances of getting interviews. You have much more to lose than to gain by stating something that could possibly backfire and reduce your chances of meeting with prospective employers.

- Providing aptitude scores and psychological test results, even if they are high. There are four reasons why you should omit information concerning testing. First, employers are primarily interested in your accomplishments; they are a better indicator of your strengths than anything else. Second, many employers are skeptical of testing due to the varying degrees of its accuracy. Third, if a company happens to be a proponent of testing, you will be evaluated by the organization prior to receiving an offer. Fourth, many employers consider it pretentious to include this kind of information. (Don't confuse stating a G.P.A. with a test result—the former is an accomplishment that's been realized through hard work.)

- Stating that you're divorced or separated. Mention that you're divorced or separated only if you're certain that it will be advantageous to be single. The obvious situation for this is when applying for a position that requires extensive travel.

- Enclosing your photograph. Due to all the legislation regarding interviewing people on only job-related matters, enclosing a photograph with your résumé is no longer an accepted practice in job hunting (unless you're working in one of those rare professions where appearance is such a key part of the job that it's actually a job-related matter, such as in modeling or the entertainment field). If there's something about you or your appearance that you want employers to know, you'll be able to convey this through one of the secondary sections in your résumé.

- Stating your date of birth, social security number, name and occupation of spouse, or number of children along with their names and ages. There's no reason to provide this information.

- Stating "Unavailable for travel," "Unavailable for relocation," and

"Unavailable for travel or relocation." Regardless of how much you don't want to relocate or travel, never state this in you résumé. You don't want to preclude yourself from being interviewed before you know how much travel is involved or where the job might be. Moreover, once a company has met you and decided that it wants to hire you, you may be able to make changes in the position if the degree of travel is objectionable or if you have to relocate. There's also the possibility that the company will want to hire you so much that it will offer you a different job, where there will be no travel or need to relocate.

• Including the names, addresses, and phone numbers of references. Don't list references even if one of them is a well-known and highly regarded individual. When job hunters tout their references, employers consider this to be pretentious and also believe that the applicants are trying to get interviews based on whom they know instead of who they are and what they've accomplished. The best thing to do is to put the statement "References furnished on request" at the end of your résumé.

• Providing salary history. Never put salary information on your résumé. Your income level may cause you to lose out on interviews because your earnings are either too high or too low. The matter of giving salary information to prospective employers in advance of an interview is discussed further in Chapter 6.

RÉSUMÉ LENGTH

Writing a résumé presents a particular challenge. You want to make the document as brief as possible, yet not at the expense of omitting important information. The shorter its length, the greater the likelihood that your résumé will be read. Interviewers balk at having to pour through reams of data in order to learn what a job hunter has to offer. Often, employers will file lengthy résumés away and eliminate the applicants from consideration.

Your résumé should never be longer than two pages, unless you have a long list of publishing or performance credits. In this case, three pages or more are acceptable.

If you've heard that a résumé should be just one page in length, that's a myth. In fact, if you have breadth and depth of experience—where you've worked for a number of companies and/or have a host of impressive accomplishments and responsibilities to discuss—a two-page résumé is actually preferable. It befits your situation. You wouldn't be expected to be able to do justice to your background using only one page.

In the event that your résumé is three pages or longer and you're having difficulty reducing it to two pages, consolidate your early employment experiences.

As an example, here's how Troy Gardner, a seasoned manager in the tennis-club business, handled his early years, 1971–1983, when he was a young man teaching tennis. Instead of stating the name and location of each employer and then listing his duties (there were actually four different employment experiences to discuss), he summed up these 12 years using only two lines of text. Here's his résumé:

Troy Gardner
6 Melbourne Place
Palm Beach, FL 33480
(407) 582-6940

OBJECTIVE

A challenging position as General Manager/Director of Tennis at a country club or sports facility seeking to increase membership, efficiency of operations, and profitability.

PROFILE

A skilled businessman and tennis professional with 23 years of progressively responsible experience in Club Management and Tennis Instruction. A history of success in increasing profitability and membership, implementing effective marketing programs, attracting and running prestigious tournaments, refurbishing and adding facilities and courts, plus developing exciting tennis programs. Consultant to the Professional Golf Association, responsible for providing expertise in all areas of tennis operations, court construction, and maintenance as well as the evaluation and review of tennis facilities throughout the P.G.A. network. Employers have included tennis clubs, country clubs, and resorts. Computer proficient.

EXPERIENCE

THE PALM BEACH TENNIS CENTER, Palm Beach, FL. 1983–present.

General Manager/Director of Tennis, 1992–present. Facility consists of 16 Har-Tru and 3 hard courts, a 25,000-square-foot clubhouse, a 300-seat dining room, plus a banquet facility, grill room, athletic center, child-care facility, and Olympic pool.

- Prepare and administer a $520,000 budget for tennis shop operations, court maintenance, plus food and beverage operations.
- Direct a staff of 23 including a Head and Assistant Tennis Professional, an Executive Chef, and a Food & Beverage Manager. Perform hiring, training, scheduling, and motivation of all personnel.
- Managed an $800,000 project consisting of renovating and reroofing the clubhouse, building a fitness center, adding 5 Har-Tru courts with championship lighting, and acquiring new kitchen equipment. Planned the athletic portion of the project and supervised all construction to ensure that quality standards, budgets, and schedules were met. Personally purchased the fitness center's athletic equipment.
- Increased membership sales from $163,000 to $370,000 through adding amenities plus creating and instituting innovative marketing programs.
- Increased tournament play by revising formats, developing scheduling techniques, and adding social activities to attract players at all levels.
- Developed and conducted numerous teaching clinics for men, ladies, and juniors.
- Assisted in operating and coordinating the Florida Twist/World Team Tennis tournament; and devised, organized, and participated in charity fund-raisers and club socials.

Director of Tennis, 1983–1992.

- Oversaw a $230,000 budget and managed 11 Har-Tru and 3 Plexi Pave courts plus the grill room and pool. Supervised a staff of 6, and developed and wrote the employee training manuals.
- Directed a $200,000 capital-improvement program including resurfacing the tennis courts, remarciting and tiling the pool, purchasing new maintenance equipment, and renovating the grounds.
- Implemented effective marketing strategies, organized tennis socials and leagues, and gave private and group lessons.
- Assisted in operating the P.G.A. Senior Chrysler Cup Golf Tournament for 5 consecutive years.

THE VENICE TENNIS CLUB, Venice, FL. 1983–1984.

Director of Tennis.

- Reversed a history of losses and stabilized the business of this stagnant 11-court tennis club.
- Increased membership from 50 to 180 through refurbishing the courts, creating and implementing programs for juniors and adults, and establishing a tennis shop.
- Due to results achieved, P.G.A. Tour took facility over. Consulted to Tournament Players Club Network, with the responsibility for setting up budgets and supervising tennis court, pool, and pro-shop construction.

1971–1983: **Head Tennis Professional** and **Associate Tennis Professional** at various clubs in Florida, South Carolina, and Georgia.

PLAYING BACKGROUND

- Awarded 4 full-year college tennis scholarships.
- #1 player on college team all 4 years.
- 1973: Florida State High School Champions—#1 in both Singles and Doubles.
- National City Team, Atlanta, GA, #2 in Singles and #1 in Doubles. 1970, 1971, 1972.

MEMBERSHIP

U.S.P.T.A. since 1981.

EDUCATION

B.A., Liberal Arts, University of Florida, 1980.

Graduate of Dale Carnegie Public Speaking Program.

Graduate of "Search of Excellence" Management Program.

Numerous management workshops through the P.G.A. Tour.

References furnished on request.

While you don't want your résumé to be too long, you also don't want it to be too brief and look empty on the page. In this instance, a background just doesn't look convincing. This is often the case with graduating students and individuals who have only a year or two of work experience.

To help make your résumé fill out the page, use ll-point type instead of 10-point and add secondary sections, such as "Strengths" and "Personal," if necessary.

Here are the before and after versions of Judy Galloway's résumé (the after version uses larger type and has had the "Strengths" section added to it):

Judy Galloway
6 Gulfway Rd.
Sarasota, FL 34242
(813) 349-3914

OBJECTIVE   Entry-level position as a Registered Nurse working on a pediatric unit.

EDUCATION   A.S., Nursing, Manatee Community College, 1995.

EXPERIENCE **SARASOTA MEMORIAL HOSPITAL**, Sarasota, FL. 1991–1993.
Phlebotomist, Outpatient Laboratory.

- Traveled to nursing homes and private homes and drew blood for tests and cultures.
- Logged specimen requests into the computer.
- Charted blood work.
- Performed PPD tests.
- Took throat cultures.

LOCKWOOD RIDGE ANIMAL CLINIC, Sarasota, FL. 1989–1991.
Veterinary Technician.

- Started IV procedures and regulated fluids.
- Assisted in surgery, including performing closure.
- Administered oral, IV, SQ, and IM medications.

References furnished on request.

Judy Galloway
6 Gulfway Rd.
Sarasota, FL 34242
(813) 349-3914

OBJECTIVE   Entry-level position as a Registered Nurse working on a pediatric unit.

EDUCATION   A.S., Nursing, Manatee Community College, 1995.

STRENGTHS
- Responsible, well organized, attentive to detail.
- An excellent communicator.
- The ability to relate with a wide variety of people.
- Work well under pressure.
- A quick thinker.
- Compassionate and understanding.

EXPERIENCE   **SARASOTA MEMORIAL HOSPITAL**, Sarasota, FL. 1991–1993.

Phlebotomist, Outpatient Laboratory.
- Traveled to nursing homes and private homes and drew blood for tests and cultures.
- Logged specimen requests into the computer.
- Charted blood work.
- Performed PPD tests.
- Took throat cultures.

LOCKWOOD RIDGE ANIMAL CLINIC, Sarasota, FL. 1989–1991.

Veterinary Technician.
- Started IV procedures and regulated fluids.
- Assisted in surgery, including performing closure.
- Administered oral, IV, SQ, and IM medications.

References furnished on request.

Another way to take up space is to change the layout of your résumé and discuss your experience *beneath* a section heading instead of *opposite* it. Here's an example, using Judy Galloway's background again. This résumé looks even better than the previous one.

Judy Galloway
6 Gulfway Rd.
Sarasota, FL 34242
(813) 349-3914

OBJECTIVE

Entry-level position as a Registered Nurse working on a pediatric unit.

EDUCATION

A.S., Nursing, Manatee Community College, 1995.

STRENGTHS

- Responsible, well organized, attentive to detail.
- An excellent communicator.
- The ability to relate with a wide variety of people.
- Work well under pressure.
- A quick thinker.
- Compassionate and understanding.

EXPERIENCE

SARASOTA MEMORIAL HOSPITAL, Sarasota, FL. 1991–1993.

Phlebotomist, Outpatient Laboratory.

- Traveled to nursing homes and private homes and drew blood for tests and cultures.
- Logged specimen requests into the computer.
- Charted blood work.
- Performed PPD tests.
- Took throat cultures.

LOCKWOOD RIDGE ANIMAL CLINIC, Sarasota, FL. 1989–1991.

Veterinary Technician.

- Started IV procedures and regulated fluids.
- Assisted in surgery, including performing closure.
- Administered oral, IV, SQ, and IM medications.

References furnished on request.

Just as you want the first page of your résumé to have a full appearance, you don't want the second page to look skimpy.

In the event that the second page consists of only one or two short sections, here's how to use up space. Put your name in the upper left-hand corner and place "Page 2" underneath it. Use bold-face type for this and skip several lines before the first section appears. Also, discuss your background beneath a section heading versus across from it (be sure you lay out the first page this way, too). Here's an example:

Annie Goetz
Page 2

COMMUNITY ACTIVITIES
> The Junior League.
> The Players Theater.

EMPLOYMENT HISTORY
> Waldenbooks, Sarasota, FL. 1991–present.
> A. Parker Books, Sarasota, FL. 1988–1991.
> Charlie's News, Sarasota, FL. 1986–1988.

> References furnished on request.

RÉSUMÉ APPEARANCE

The appearance of your résumé is as important as its content.

If your résumé is attractive to the eye, prospective employers will automatically begin to read it, and with enthusiasm. However, if your résumé looks like you gave it only a half-hearted effort, then most employers will immediately rule you out. They'll assume that you give your job a half-hearted effort as well, and they won't want to waste their time interviewing you. After all, when trying to get interviews, if you're not willing to give something as important as your résumé a 100% effort, how important can your job and career really be to you?

To ensure that the appearance of your résumé is a door-opening asset—and not a liability—here's how to proceed.

EQUIPMENT

Your finished résumé should be laser printed. Hopefully, you have a computer with laser printer at home. If not, when you've completed your final draft, take your handwritten or typed résumé to a secretarial service. They all have laser printers.

Never try to save money by typing your résumé and then photocopying it. A typed résumé is regarded by many employers as having put forth only a cursory effort.

TYPE STYLE AND SIZE

Select a conservative style of type that will lend dignity to your résumé plus make it easy to read. Fancy or exotic type is appropriate only for positions in extremely creative fields. It's best to use Helvetica or one of the Roman styles. The résumés in this book are set in Helvetica.

As far as type size is concerned, it can range from 10-point to ll-point. A smaller size will make many readers squint, and a larger size will look childish.

MARGINS

For the best eye appeal, prepare your résumé with 1" margins on all four sides of the page. However, if you happen to need just a tad more space to make your résumé fit onto one or two pages, then it's acceptable to make the top margin 3/4" and the bottom margin 1/2".

WHITE SPACE

It's important to have a good deal of white space on your résumé. These are the portions of the document where there's no text whatsoever. It's especially important to have ample white space between your letterhead and the first section as well as between each of the sections that follows. This way the sections will stand out and your résumé will be easy to read. If your résumé is overrun with words and has a crammed look, no one will want to deal with it.

Never produce a résumé like either of the two that follow. Todd Alexander enables his résumé to fit onto one page by removing all the spacing between his different jobs and descriptions of his duties.

Frank Connelley manages to preserve the white space on his résumé, but this is at the expense of using type that's so small that many people will have to squint in order to read it.

Todd Alexander
5 Heron's Court
Sarasota, FL 34232
(813) 377-7208

PROFILE   An accomplished Attorney with extensive administrative and technical experience in land-title insurance and real-estate appraisals and closings. The author of numerous real-estate articles and opinions published by national, state, and local newspapers and professional organizations, including the American Bar Journal, *Chicago Tribune*, and newsletter of the Illinois Bar Association.

EXPERIENCE   PRIVATE PRACTICE, Chicago, IL. 1976–1996.
Attorney.
- Specialized in residential real-estate closings, primarily for condominiums, small apartment buildings, and private homes.
- Proficient in metes and bounds legal descriptions.
- Member of Chicago Bar Association and active member of real-estate subcommittee. Reviewed proposed real-estate legislation and made recommendations on bills.
- An officer of Midwest Appraisal Company, a firm that specialized in appraising commercial, apartment, industrial, and office buildings nationwide.

CAPITAL TELEPHONE, INC., Milwaukee, WI. 1974–1976.
Finance Attorney.
- Directed programs to resolve interim financial needs of operating companies.
- Evaluated economic feasibility and legality of financial strategies.
- Reviewed and recommended alternative methods of medium-and long-term financing for corporate holding company.
- Developed procedure enabling Wisconsin public utilities to issue exempt 360-day, intrastate notes. Also established department that sold the notes.

ROYAL NEIGHBORS OF AMERICA, Rock Island, IL. 1972–1974.
Assistant General Counsel-Investment Department for this fraternal life insurance company. Reported to Board of Directors each month.
- Confirmed legality of company investments and conducted ancillary research.
- Clarified investment terms with counsel and brokers nationwide.

PIONEER NATIONAL TITLE INSURANCE COMPANY, Chicago, IL. 1970–1972.
Assistant Regional Counsel-Law Department.
- Counseled clients and company personnel on real-estate title problems.
- Improved research procedures to reduce claims. Also created guidelines to minimize operational errors.
- Researched claims and reviewed tax-deed proceedings.

CHICAGO TITLE AND TRUST COMPANY, Chicago, IL. 1962–1970.
Attorney in Title Legal Department.
- Managed regional office for a 29-county area.
- Specialized in real-estate tax and assessment problems.

GARBER AND FRASER, Chicago, IL. 1960–1962.
Attorney.
- Assisted Real-Estate Partner in real-estate tax and assessment matters.
- Conducted research on special projects.

EDUCATION   Juris Doctor, Ohio State University, 1960.
B.A., Political Science, Ohio State University, 1958.

Frank Connelley
6 Rhodes Drive
West Palm Beach, FL 33480
(407) 588-0909

PROFILE

14 years of progressively responsible positions and a track record of accomplishments in automated Warehouse/Distribution Management. Have closed warehouses, planned and set up new facilities, increased operating efficiencies, and reduced costs. An excellent manager and motivator of personnel. Warehouses have been both union and nonunion.

EXPERIENCE

WILDER BROTHERS, INC., West Palm Beach, FL. 1986–present.

Vice President of Operations for this full-line Toro distributor of wholegoods and parts for lawn equipment and irrigation systems. Direct a staff of 20, including 3 managers, with complete responsibility for shipping/receiving, warehousing, inventory control, parts marketing, traffic/distribution, and maintenance at this 67,000-square-foot facility with annual sales in excess of $23,000,000.

- Recipient of "Mr. Parts" award from Toro Corporation twice in the last 5 years. Designated #1 in the country for performance out of 52 distributors nationwide.
- Managed the Operations Division under budget each year since 1990.
- Closed 2 warehouses and planned the layout, material-handling needs, and space allocation for this centrally located facility.
- Achieved a 100% freight-claims-recovery success-rate with trucklines.
- Plan the operating budget, perform fleet-lease negotiations, create and implement marketing strategies for selling parts, and decide the products to purchase and stock in order to provide maximum customer-service levels and turns.

BEALL'S DEPARTMENT STORES, Bradenton, FL. 1982–1986.

Company operated a 33-unit junior department store chain and a 10-store subsidiary chain. Annual sales: $95,000,000.

Distribution Director of this new 113,000-square-foot computerized/conveyorized distribution center.

- Planned the move into this new facility and directed it without disruption of operations.
- Managed 3 Assistant Managers, 19 Supervisors, and 250 hourly employees on 2 shifts.
- Reduced incoming freight costs by 80%.
- Was instrumental in devising productivity gains that enabled the distribution center to handle growth from 24 to 43 stores without hiring additional personnel.
- Personally performed the Purchasing, Traffic, and Fleet functions.

JEFFERSON-WARD, Orlando, FL. 1980–1982.

Company operated a 48-unit department store chain.

Operations Manager of this new 240,000-square-foot distribution center.

- Planned the warehouse and set up operations.
- Managed 7 Supervisors and 150 employees.
- Previous positions included **Operations Manager, Transfer Manager, Receiving Manager, Supervisor of Break Bulk Area,** and **Executive Trainee,** all at a 212,000-square-foot distribution center in Miami.

EDUCATION

B.S., Business Administration, University of Florida, 1980.

CONTRAST

So that your résumé will have an attractive and balanced appearance and your name and the different sections will stand out, use bold-face type and capital letters as follows:

Set your name in your letterhead in bold-face type. Also make it one point-size larger than the type for the balance of your letterhead and résumé.

Set the section headings in type that's both bold-face and capitalized.

If you're using the chronological format, put the names of your employers in capital letters, using either bold- or regular-face type.

Never use underlining, italics, shadows, boxes, or decorative borders. Today, an increasing number of companies are using computer scanners to review résumés, and many scanners cannot read words that have been underlined, that are set in italics, that are close to borders, or that are in boxes or in shaded areas. These résumés are automatically rejected.

After you've completed the first draft of your résumé, go through it and ask yourself these questions:

Does my résumé convincingly convey my capability to perform the kind of work that I want to do?

Does my résumé accurately convey what my responsibilities have been?

Does the document express my most important accomplishments and duties?

Are my statements short, crisp, and to the point?

Are there any negatives or liabilities in my background that I need to remove or minimize?

Are there any things I can do to improve my résumé to make my qualifications stronger?

For each piece of information you've offered, ask yourself:

What does this say about me?

What does this not say about me?

What does this imply?

After considering these questions, make the necessary changes. While improving your résumé, be sure to check on spelling, punctuation, and grammar. Then put your résumé down and don't look at it for a day or two.

When you read your résumé again, don't be surprised if it doesn't convey your background as well as you thought it would and that you want to make more changes. Before your résumé will achieve the level you want, expect to rewrite it several times. Continue this process of reviewing and fine-tuning your résumé, then putting it down for a while, until you're completely satisfied with what you've written.

Once your résumé is at the level you want, show it to other people for their comments and suggestions. The document may not read to others the way you think it does. You'll get the most useful feedback from people who work in your field and have an in-depth knowledge of the work that you do.

PROOFREADING

If you're going to have your résumé printed by a secretarial service or commercial printer, it's important that you first proofread their work. It's rare for mistakes not to be made. Also, do the proofreading at home, not in the printer's office. The task is harder than it appears because the tendency is to read complete words, not individual letters. If you read your résumé *backwards,* you'll catch errors you would otherwise miss. Proofread for layout as well as for spelling and punctuation.

STOCK

Select high-quality stock; the recommended weight is 24 pounds. Good colors to use are off-white, ivory, light beige, and light gray. Don't try to gain a reader's attention by using shocking colors such as pink, lavender, lime, lemon, or purple unless you're pursuing a position in an artistic field.

Purchase extra sheets of paper for your cover letters and buy matching envelopes.

Once the printing has been done, if your résumé is two pages in length, staple the pages together. If you have reason to believe that some of the companies you'll be sending your résumé to will be using a computer scanner for reading your résumé, save some copies that have *not* been stapled together. Mail these copies *unfolded* in an 8" x 11" envelope. Computer scanners have difficulty reading the text that's near a fold line.

CHAPTER 5

SPECIAL TIPS, SPECIAL SITUATIONS, AND SPECIAL JOB HUNTERS

This section contains the finishing touches for writing your résumé.

Although the majority of the information won't apply to your particular situation, some of it will—and these tips will be invaluable for strengthening your qualifications and enhancing your résumé. Key information is also provided for the career changer, the graduating student, and the housewife who is reentering the work force. Each of these individuals faces a unique set of challenges for conveying their background and qualifications to prospective employers.

SPECIAL TIPS

THE PROFILE

As explained on page 7, a profile can do much more than substitute for a job objective. Below are five key roles it can perform.

While including a profile is effective in both the functional and chronological résumés, it has a greater impact in the chronological since this type of résumé lacks the functional's exceptional ability to shape a background and highlight important information. The examples will therefore utilize the chronological approach.

1. **Convey Multiple Strengths**

If you have multiple strengths in a particular field, you'll probably want prospective employers to know about this right off the bat. The best way to convey this information is through stating it in a profile. This will ensure that your background will be considered for the various positions that require these strengths.

To illustrate this approach, here's the résumé of Tom Merriman. Tom has eight years' experience in the cabinet business, with expertise in marketing and production, the two areas of his field that he wants prospective employers to know he's an expert in. Tom would accept a good offer performing either of these activities.

Thomas D. Merriman
2 Fairway Drive
Sarasota, FL 34243
(813) 359-5250

PROFILE

8 years' experience in the Marketing and Production of multiunit and custom cabinetry for kitchens, baths, and wall units. A track record of success in increasing sales, decreasing production costs, and boosting production output.

EXPERIENCE

EUROPEAN KITCHENS & BATH, Sarasota FL. 1991–present.

Sales Representative for this company that designs, produces, and installs European-style cabinetry for both remodeling and new construction. Offer custom work as well as a standard line.

- Tripled territory sales in the past 6 years.
- Call on builders of homes in the Bradenton-Sarasota-Venice market. Also meet with homeowners at company showroom and at their residence.
- Determine clients' needs and suggest layouts and designs to satisfy their tastes and specifications.
- Prepare quotations and follow up to close business.
- Design and write all copy for advertisements, brochures, and point-of-sale material.

BEST CABINET CORPORATION, Sarasota, FL. 1984–1989.

Sales Representative, 1988–1989, for this company that designed and produced a standard line of European-style cabinetry.

- Called on builders of apartments and condominiums.
- Designed layouts to meet with company's standard-line specifications.
- Prepared quotations and followed up to generate orders.

Production Supervisor, 1986–1988.

- Directed up to 50 people, with complete responsibility for production, quality control, job training, and safety.
- Reduced production time by 25% and decreased material costs by 10%.
- Eliminated 7 jobs, requiring 10 fewer people on the payroll.
- 1984–1986, held rotating assignments in the factory and performed every job in cabinet production.

EDUCATION

A.S., Architectural & Building Construction, Manatee Community College, 1991.

2. Convey Qualifications for a Diverse Job Objective

A profile can be used to convey the ability to perform a job objective that states an interest in two totally unrelated positions. An additional advantage of using a résumé containing this profile is that it will enable you to conduct your job search with one résumé instead of two.

Let's use the background of Lynn Haupt as an example. In Lynn's first résumé, she states that she wants to be an accountant or a private investigator. These two jobs have nothing to do with each other, and many employers will be skeptical of Lynn upon learning that she's interested in two totally unrelated types of work. Some will immediately reject her, preferring an applicant who has more focus and career direction. This will particularly be the case with employers who are seeking an accountant, since Lynn begins her résumé by amplifying on her investigation background.

Lynn's second résumé (only the first page is shown) contains a profile that explains that she has 21 years' combined experience in these two fields. It now makes perfect sense for Lynn to be pursuing a position either as an accountant or as a private investigator. There is every reason to interview her, and for either position. Here are Lynn's résumés:

Lynn Haupt
18 Garden Circle
Sarasota, FL 34243
(813) 346-5630

OBJECTIVE

A challenging position as an Accountant or Private Investigator.

EXPERIENCE

SIMMONS & ASSOCIATES, INC., Sarasota, FL. 1993–present.

Office Manager/Private Investigator for this investigative-services firm. Possess "A" License, #93002119, and am a Licensed Process Server, #01879, Twelfth Judicial Circuit Court.

Investigative Responsibilities

- Perform investigations plus direct and coordinate the daily activities of up to 5 other investigators.

- Brief clients on all investigations and information obtained.

- Services include:

  -Surveillance. Accurately document the subject's activities, utilizing the latest in high-tech video and photographic equipment and surveillance techniques.

  -Employee Monitoring. Observe and report to client the employee's activities and behavior.

  -Activity Checks. Perform discreet neighborhood interviews and analysis of the subject's day-to-day capabilities, physical condition, surroundings, and lifestyle.

  -Locates. Determine location of subject, utilizing an extensive network of local, state, and national sources.

  -Backgrounds. Conduct detailed investigation into subject's background and provide a complete view of subject's criminal, civil, and driving history.

  -Assets. Provide a comprehensive review of financial sources and courthouse records to identify tangible assets, including information regarding both real and personal property.

Accounting/Bookkeeping Responsibilities

- Perform accounting/bookkeeping duties including accounts receivable and payable, payroll and taxes, bank reconciliations, general ledgers, trial balances, spreadsheets, plus monthly, quarterly, and annual P&L statements.

- Prepare correspondence and maintain records and files.

- Converted data bank from manual to computerized storage.

Lynn Haupt
Page 2

FLORIDA CLAIMS BUREAU, INC., Sarasota, FL. 1991–1993.

Investigator-C License #9200516.

- Performed surveillances, activity checks, locates, background checks, asset determinations, and employee monitoring.

HAUPT ACCOUNTING, Sarasota, FL. 1984–1991.

Owner/Operator of this accounting service.

- Performed accounting, bookkeeping, and income tax preparation for 65 clients, including individuals and corporations.

- Key activities consisted of preparing monthly financial statements, including reconciliation of journals, general ledger, and spreadsheets for sales analyses and productivity reports; payroll, including quarterly reports for retirement plans and state and federal taxes; sales-tax reports; state and federal income tax returns for individuals, partnerships, and corporations.

REED, DERRINGER, PLATH & ASSOCIATES, INC., Sarasota, FL. 1980–1984.

Accountant at this C.P.A. firm.

SKINNER EXCAVATION & SNOW REMOVAL, Dillon, CO. 1975–1980.

Accountant and **Office Manager**.

COMPUTER SKILLS

Proficient in WordPerfect 5.1., Lotus 1-2-3, and Vertical Market Software.

EDUCATION

B.A., Accounting, University of Colorado, 1975.

References furnished on request.

Lynn Haupt
18 Garden Circle
Sarasota, FL 34243
(813) 346-5630

OBJECTIVE

A challenging position as an Accountant or Private Investigator.

PROFILE

A degreed Accountant and Licensed Private Investigator with 21 years' combined experience in the fields. Financial background includes Accounting and Bookkeeping services. Investigative skills include Surveillances, Employee Monitoring, Activity Checks, Locates, Backgrounds, and Assets.

EXPERIENCE

SIMMONS & ASSOCIATES, INC., Sarasota, FL. 1993–present.

Office Manager/Private Investigator at this investigative-services firm. Possess "A" License, #93002119, and am a Licensed Process Server, #01879, Twelfth Judicial Circuit Court.

Investigative Responsibilities

- Perform investigations plus direct and coordinate the daily activities of up to 5 other investigators.
- Brief clients on all investigations and information obtained.
- Services include:

  -Surveillance. Accurately document the subject's activities, utilizing the latest in high-tech video and photographic equipment and surveillance techniques.

  -Employee Monitoring. Observe and report to client the employee's activities and behavior.

  -Activity Checks. Perform discreet neighborhood interviews and analysis of the subject's day-to-day capabilities, physical condition, surroundings, and lifestyle.

  -Locates. Determine location of subject, utilizing an extensive network of local, state, and national sources.

  -Backgrounds. Conduct detailed investigation into subject's background and provide a complete view of subject's criminal, civil, and driving history.

  -Assets. Provide a comprehensive review of financial sources and courthouse records to identify tangible assets, including information regarding both real and personal property.

3. **Highlight Key Background Information**

A profile can be used to instantly convey something about you that you believe will make a highly favorable impression on all readers.

Let's take a look at two examples. The first is the profile of Susan Symington. Susan is seeking a senior-level position either in financial management or operations, however she wants to leave the museum field and go to work for a hospital or some other health-care facility. Because Susan has never worked in the health field before, she wants employers to know that she is a registered nurse, which means that she is very familiar with how health-care organizations operate. The fact that Susan has an M.B.A. is an added plus.

The second example is the background of Stacy Moran. Stacy is an elementary-school teacher and has been featured on television three times for her teaching skills. This is an accomplishment that will impress everyone who reads the profile in her résumé.

Susan Symington
3678 Countryside Lane
Sarasota, FL 34233
(813) 925-5398

OBJECTIVE

A challenging operations/financial management responsibility with a growing health-care organization.

CAREER SUMMARY

An R.N. and M.B.A. with a track record of success in managing the financial, administrative, and business functions of a nationally recognized museum. Restructured and streamlined operations, increased operating efficiencies, created new revenue-producing departments, and reduced costs. An excellent short-and long-range planner, as well as published author on financial management.

EXPERIENCE

THE GULF COAST MUSEUM OF ART, Sarasota, FL. 1986–1996.

Deputy Director for Business and Administration, 1989–1996. Reported to the CEO with complete responsibility for managing the financial, administrative, and business functions: accounting, personnel, admissions, purchasing, security, buildings, grounds, gift shop, and restaurant. Directed 83 people including 8 managers.

- Established museum policies and developed short-and long-range plans in conjunction with the Director and Board of Trustees.
- Lobbied Florida legislature for the appropriation of state funds.
- Restructured and streamlined the departments of accounting, personnel, security, buildings, and the restaurant, resulting in increased operating efficiencies, lower costs, and compliance with federal law and industry standards.
- Responsible for financial planning and a $5,000,000 budget. Also decentralized budget control to include department heads' participation and accountability. Result was goal-orientation and greater control over expenditures.
- Established the management policy and guidelines for the museum's $1,200,000 investment fund. Also monitored compliance of government and foundation grants.
- Designed and instituted a facilities rental program, generating up to $35,000 a year in profits.
- Turned a $70,000 annual loss into a $50,000 annual profit by terminating service contract and converting restaurant to a staff-run operation.

Chief Financial Officer, 1987–1989.

- Managed the administrative and financial functions including public, private, and restricted funds. Also managed the museum's investments.

- Coordinated budget preparation, monitored variances, and analyzed the overall financial status of the museum.
- Acted as liaison between the museum and the Department of State's Office of Planning and Budgeting for the acquisition of state funds. Also monitored funded projects to ensure compliance with restrictions and regulations.
- Established maintenance schedules for buildings and grounds, and reviewed all contracts, insurance policies, and legal documents.

Financial Analyst, 1986–1987.

- Designed and implemented a computerized accounting system and formal budgeting and reporting system.
- Developed procedures for tracking expenses for a $20,000,000 fixed capital repair and restoration program.
- Created a fund-accounting structure for restricted gifts and grants.
- Analyzed financial performance of revenue-producing operations including membership, merchandise, fairs, festivals, and food service.
- Provided financial data for grant budgets and grant reporting.

UNIVERSITY OF FLORIDA GRADUATE SCHOOL OF BUSINESS, Gainesville, FL. 1985–1986.

Graduate Assistant. Assisted in the publication of financial management textbooks. Coauthored *Fundamentals of Financial Management Study Guide*, Fourth Edition, CBS Publishing. 1985.

EDUCATION

M.B.A., Finance, University of Florida Graduate School of Business, 1986.
B.A., Sociology, Webster University, 1984.
R.N. Diploma, Barnes Hospital School of Nursing, 1982.

References furnished on request.

Stacy Moran
6005 Midnight Cove Lane
Sarasota, FL 34242
(813) 349-4179

OBJECTIVE   Teacher at the Elementary-School level.

PROFILE   17 years' experience teaching in elementary schools, both in regular and special programs. Teaching skills and classroom activities have been featured on local television news shows 3 separate times. Strengths include leadership, organizational, and communication skills, as well as the ability to create a classroom environment conducive to learning.

EXPERIENCE   ALTA VISTA ELEMENTARY SCHOOL, Sarasota, FL. 1985–1996.

Teacher, 2nd Grade Regular Education-1990–1996.

Teacher, 2nd Grade Chapter 1-1987–1990.

Paraprofessional Aide-1985–1987.
• Worked in EH/SLD/VE programs, grades K–5.

• Taught a wide range of math and reading subjects.

ACTIVITIES:

Wrote and produced a historical play for the school's 40th anniversary, 1994. Trained students in their roles and coordinated costuming and presentations.

Selected to be Presenter and Facilitator at Core Knowledge Conference, Miami, FL, 1993.

Core Knowledge Committee, 1991–1994.

Science-Fair Committee, 1985–1994. Chairperson, 1994.

Grade Chairperson, 1989–1993.

Student-Council Sponsor, 1989–1992.

Faculty Council, 1988.

Hospitality Committee, 1986–1987.

SARASOTA COUNTY SCHOOL BOARD, Sarasota, FL. 1984–1985.

Substitute Teacher.

Previously, taught kindergarten at Julie Rohr Academy in Sarasota, FL (1981–1983), taught pre-K, 1, and 2 at Duette Elementary School in Duette, FL (1980–1981), and taught kindergarten at Elkin King Elementary School in Bainbridge, GA (1979–1980).

EDUCATION   B.S., Elementary Education, Florida State University, 1978.

4. Highlight Early Work Experience

Sometimes job hunters have work experience that took place early in their career that's more pertinent to the position they're seeking than their most recent position is. An excellent way to bring forth this part of a background is to describe it in a profile.

Patti Hoffman was interested in going to work for a resort hotel as director of marketing. Because her jobs at Coastal Publications and Inter-Travel had nothing to do with this position and the work she performed at Carib-Resort did, she highlighted her Carib-Resort experience in her profile.

Patti Hoffman
82 The Breezes
Lantana, FL 33462
(407) 588-1302

OBJECTIVE   Director of Marketing for a resort hotel.

PROFILE   A trilingual world traveler with a track record of accomplishments in marketing vacation packages to resort hotels. Background includes managing up to 50 people as well as training over 100 travel agents. An innovative and energetic marketer with the proven ability to train, motivate, and direct personnel.

EXPERIENCE   COASTAL PUBLICATIONS, INC., West Palm Beach, FL. 1995–present.
Branch Manager.

Opened up branch and started this business that publishes an annual leisure/dining directory containing over 500 local merchants. Manage a staff of 9.

- Achieved first-year revenues of over $500,000.
- Hired and trained all marketing and administrative personnel.
- Recruited and trained nonprofit organizations to sell the directory.
- Personally designed and laid out directory and oversaw its production.

INTER-TRAVEL, INC., New York, NY. 1991–1995.
Manager of this travel agency.

- Oversaw all departments of this $8,000,000 operation and supervised a staff of 12.
- Increased productivity through restructuring internal operations and systems plus automating and upgrading skills and work habits of travel consultants.
- Created and instituted a quality-control system.
- Saved company significant sums of money by reducing staff, cross training, and redistributing the work load.

CARIB-RESORT, INC., Washington, D.C. 1981–1991.
Director of Product Development. 1988–1991.

One of the initial 3 people who started this vacation-package business that marketed trips to resorts in the Caribbean, Mexico, and Europe.

- Built annual revenues to $25,000,000 in 4 years.
- Visited resort hotels and negotiated rates; also negotiated rates with airlines and ground operators. Then structured vacation packages.

Patti Hoffman
Page 2

- Compiled and published a quarterly magazine that was mailed to 2,200,000 travel-club members.
- Trained over 100 travel agents to sell the resort-vacation packages.

Previous positions included **Manager of Quality Control** for the Travel Division, **Manager of Leisure Sales, Sales Trainer,** and **Travel Agent**.

EDUCATION   B.A., American University, 1981.
    Major: Communications.
    Minor: Marketing and Business.

PERSONAL   Fluent in French and Spanish. Have traveled extensively throughout the world. Born in Paris, France.

References furnished on request.

5. **Highlight Important Personal Qualities**

Occasionally, job hunters will have certain personal qualities that will be important for the work they're seeking and that will enhance their qualifications for this position. These attributes can be readily conveyed through a profile.

Jorge Rodriguez had just received his A.S. degree in nursing and wanted to work as a registered nurse in an emergency room or critical-care setting. This is a position that usually requires two or three years' experience due to the life-or-death nature of the duties being performed.

To help offset his lack of experience, Jorge included a profile in which he stated important personal qualities that would convey his ability to handle this demanding position.

Jorge Rodriguez
2549 Hawthorne St.
Sarasota, FL 34239
(813) 957-2968

OBJECTIVE   Position as a Registered Nurse working in an Emergency Room or Critical-Care setting.

PROFILE   Recently received A.S. in Nursing, with 10 years' previous experience in the medical field, as a cardiovascular technologist and phlebotomist in civilian life and hospital corpsman in the U.S. Navy. A quick thinker with the proven ability to remain calm under pressure and handle multiple tasks simultaneously.

EDUCATION   A.S., Nursing, Manatee Community College, 1995.

Certificate, Cardiovascular Technician, Baptist Medical Center, 1991.

Certificate, Hospital Corpsman, U.S. Navy Hospital Corps School, 1989.

EXPERIENCE   **SARASOTA MEMORIAL HOSPITAL**, Sarasota, FL. 1991–present.
Cardiovascular Technologist.

- Prepare patients for invasive procedures.
- Assist physicians in cardiovascular procedures.
- Utilize state-of-the-art medical equipment.

BAPTIST MEDICAL CENTER, Montgomery, AL. 1989–1991.
Phlebotomist/Lab Clerk.

- Logged specimen requests into computer.
- Drew blood and charted blood work.

U.S. NAVY, San Diego, CA. 1985–1989.
Hospital Corpsman.

- Assisted in minor surgery.
- Worked in maternity/labor, delivery, and newborn nursery.
- Ordered supplies and maintained health records.

References furnished on request.

THE OBJECTIVE/PROFILE COMBINATION

A further way to highlight information about yourself is to include in your job objective information that would normally appear in a profile.

This technique is particularly useful when what you want to say is so brief that it can be stated in a single sentence. While a one-sentence profile would look rather skimpy on a résumé, when this information is combined with the job objective, it makes for a convincing statement of the position being sought. Recent graduates, who lack in-depth experience and therefore aren't able to write comprehensive, accomplishments-filled profiles, often benefit from this approach. The résumé of Brian O'Malley serves as an example.

Brian C. O'Malley
116 Spring Lane
Bradenton, FL 34209
(813) 756-2208

OBJECTIVE   An entry-level position in Production Management with a growing company, providing the opportunity to learn a field and build a career. Seeking to utilize recent degree in Management plus work experience in Inventory Control, Purchasing, and Employee Training/Scheduling.

EDUCATION   B.S., Business Administration, University of Central Florida, Orlando, FL. 1995.
Major: Management.

Key courses included Production/Operation Management, Service Management, Strategic Management, Personnel Management, and International Management.

Paid for 50% of college education through working at Publix Super Markets.

STRENGTHS   • A team player who works well with a wide variety of people.

• Well organized with excellent follow-through.

• Hardworking and goal-driven.

COMPUTER   Software: Microsoft Excel 4.0; WordPerfect 6.0; Lotus 1-2-3;
SKILLS   Microsoft Word 6.0; DBASE III.

Languages: DOS, Basic Programming.

EXPERIENCE   **PUBLIX SUPER MARKETS, INC.**, Orlando and Sarasota, FL. 1988–1995.

Produce Clerk, Orlando, 1993–1995.

• Cited by Management for excellence in performance.

• Responsible for inventory control. Ensured that sufficient daily inventory was on hand. Called other units as needed to replenish supplies. Also ordered and purchased products and supplies.

• Assisted Produce Manager in setting employees' schedules based on projected sales per man-hour.

• Trained Produce Clerks in Publix policies and operating procedures.

• Assisted customers with purchase needs and various inquiries.

Produce Clerk/Stockman, Sarasota, 1988–1993.

• Assisted Produce Manager in ordering supplies.

• Assisted customers and filled special orders for them.

• Constructed displays.

Special Situations

HONORS AND AWARDS

If you're fortunate enough to have received numerous honors and awards for the work you've done, this information should appear early in your résumé, certainly before you describe your work experience. Nothing will be a stronger indicator of your expertise than these accolades. Anyone who receives your résumé will read it with enthusiasm.

Tony Delvecchio is an excellent example of such a job hunter. Here's his résumé:

Tony Delvecchio
5726 Cortez Road West
Bradenton, FL 34210
(813) 794-3985

OBJECTIVE

Food & Beverage Manager at a full-service restaurant or hotel dining room.

PROFILE

A graduate of the Culinary Institute of America with a career of success in the restaurant business. The recipient of numerous honors and awards for Restaurant Quality, Chef Instruction, as well as Chef. Have opened and managed new restaurants plus directed operations at existing facilities. Possess multi-unit experience.

HONORS AND AWARDS

- "Best Seafood Restaurant in 1990"—cited by readers of *Connecticut Magazine*.
- Three-Star Award—*Hartford Courant*, 1990.
- "Favorite New Restaurant"—*Vernon, Connecticut Journal Enquirer*, 1989.
- "1979 Chef of the Year-Connecticut"—Associated Restaurants of Connecticut.
- "Outstanding Chef Instructor, 1970"—Associated Restaurants of Connecticut.
- Co-Chairman/Chef, Annual Associated Restaurants of Connecticut Gourmet Dinner for "Outstanding Restauranteurs," 1969 and 1970.

CAREER SUMMARY

- As General Manager and Executive Chef, have planned, laid out, designed, opened, and managed restaurants and hotel/cruise-ship dining rooms seating from 50 to 2,500 persons. Facilities have comprised fine dining, fine seafood dining, casual seafood, casual American, and New England clam bake.
- Generated annual revenues of up to $3,200,000.
- Recruited, hired, trained, and motivated staffs of up to 100 people, including 9 supervisors.
- Simultaneously managed 2 dining rooms, 4 kitchens, a kitchen staff of 60, plus the banquet function.
- Wrote job descriptions for all employees plus employee manuals.
- Contracted for all services, selected vendors, plus purchased required equipment, furniture, fixtures, and supplies.
- Planned and designed menus, and set up recipes for uniformity in cooking.

- Established cost and inventory control systems.
- Operated catering and mobile catering facilities that fed up to 15,000 customers daily.
- Managed restaurants that were open 24 hours a day, 7 days a week.
- Served as Food & Beverage Director at a boarding school.
- Taught food-services course

EDUCATION

Associates Degree, Culinary Institute of America, Hyde Park, NY. 1980.

Certificate, Culinary Institute of America, Hyde Park, NY. 1955.

EMPLOYMENT HISTORY

The Harborside, Longboat Key, FL. 1995–1996. Executive Chef.
Delvecchio's, Sturbridge, MA. 1991–1995. Owner/General Manager.
Chowdertown Restaurant, Vernon, CT. 1988–1991. Owner/Chef.
Delvecchio's Catering, Vernon, CT. 1981–1990. Owner/Operator.
Howard Johnson's Conference Center, Windsor Locks, CT. 1980–1981. Executive Chef.
Hartford Hilton Hotel, Hartford, CT. 1978–1980. Executive Chef.
Holiday Inn, East Hartford, CT. 1976–1978. Executive Chef.
American Cruise Lines, E. Haddam, CT. 1976. Executive Chef.
Avon Old Farms School, Avon, CT. 1973–1976. Food & Beverage Director.
Connecticut State Department of Vocational Education, Middletown, CT. 1971–1973. Chef Instructor.
Associated Restaurants of Connecticut, Hartford, CT. 1968–1971. Chef Instructor.
Bernice's Restaurant, Guilford, CT. 1960–1968. Chef/Manager.

References furnished on request.

THE FACT THAT YOU'VE BEEN RECRUITED

Another wonderful testimonial to your expertise is the fact that you've been recruited out of a company by a professional associate. It's particularly impressive when this individual was a former manager. No one could possibly have a better understanding of your capabilities.

Eugene Slattery had the good fortune to have been recruited twice, the first time by an individual at the State of Alabama Highway Department and the second time by someone at his current employer, Pavex. He makes sure that this appears on his résumé.

Eugene D. Slattery
80 Oak Drive
St. Petersburg, FL 33702
(813) 579-2480

PROFILE

A Registered Professional Engineer with 13 years' progressively responsible experience in roadway construction and bridge replacement. An outstanding manager and motivator of personnel with the proven ability to complete projects on schedule and within budget. Hardworking, goal-driven, cost-conscious.

PROFESSIONAL EXPERIENCE

PAVEX CORPORATION, Tampa, FL. 1992–present.

Branch Manager.

Was recruited out of previous company by President of Pavex. Hold complete responsibility for managing this $15,000,000 branch engaged in the business of heavy highway construction, asphalt production, and the mining of roadway materials. Key duties consist of:

MANAGEMENT OF ESTIMATES

• Oversee 3 Project Managers. Personally review all projects being bid, both public and private.

• Prepare asphalt plant estimates for use in bids as well as in sales to other construction companies.

• Establish bidding guidelines for crew size, production rates, equipment allocation, and material sources.

MANAGEMENT OF FIELD FORCES

• Direct construction crews consisting of 2 Superintendents, 10 Foremen, and approximately 50 hourly workers. Activities include scheduling and construction sequencing.

• Responsible for 2 asphalt plants. Manage 2 Foremen and oversee the types of mixes and designs.

• Resolve all construction problems, such as workmanship, proper materials, equipment, crews, subcontractors, and plans/specs disputes.

OFFICE ADMINISTRATION

• Review invoices and approve for payment. Also prepare billings.

• Create monthly reports for Corporate Office. Items include revenues, P&L, status of current projects, and current bid activity.

• Review computer reports pertaining to managing branch and its costs.

SURFACE INDUSTRIES, Bradenton, FL. 1987–1992.

Company was in the business of roadway construction.

Assistant Branch Manager, 1991–1992.

- Assisted the Vice President in branch operations. Responsibilities included managing field forces plus handling receivables and payables.

Estimator/Project Manager, 1989–1991.

- Brought roadway and site-development projects to contract. Jobs ranged from $50,000 to $1,500,000.
- Previous positions included **Superintendent, Quality Assurance Technician,** and **Grade Foreman**.

STATE OF ALABAMA HIGHWAY DEPARTMENT, Mobile, AL. 1985–1987.

Office Engineer.

- Was recruited out of previous company by current manager.
- Worked on 4 federally funded projects ranging in cost from $4,000,000 to $65,000,000.

BALDWIN COUNTY HIGHWAY DEPARTMENT, Bay Minette, AL. 1984–1985.

County Engineer-Trainee.

- Worked on 8 state- or federally-funded projects ranging from bridge replacement to new roadway construction.

CALHOUN COUNTY HIGHWAY DEPARTMENT, Anniston, AL. 1983–1984.

Assistant County Engineer.

- Obtained state and federal monies for bridge replacement and resurfacing projects.

EDUCATION

B.S., Civil Engineering, University of Alabama, 1983.
Registered Professional Engineer, Florida, 1989.

ORGANIZATIONS

Florida Engineering Society.
National Society of Professional Engineers.
University of Alabama Alumni Association.
Christian Education and Youth Group Leader.

References furnished on request.

LETTERS OF RECOMMENDATION

Many job hunters have received glowing letters of recommendation from previous managers, and their remarks can be effectively woven into a résumé by including them in a profile.

These statements give enormous credibility to a job hunter's background. They also add flavor to their résumé since so few job hunters use this approach.

Here's how Audrey Stram incorporated portions of letters of recommendation into her profile (only page one of her résumé appears):

Audrey S. Stram
18 Oak St.
Venice, FL 34292
(813) 483-2581

OBJECTIVE   Dental Assistant for a dentist in private practice.

PROFILE   Over 10 years' experience as a Dental Assistant. Background includes Operatory, Laboratory, and Front-Office duties. Selected by American Red Cross to receive the first award ever given at my facility for "Outstanding Service" in dental assistance. In addition:

-described as "fantastic dental assistant who is extremely competent in all phases of dentistry."

-cited for having "flawless work performance" over a 3-year period.

-deemed "a terrific personality that puts the most apprehensive person at ease."

-awarded "Red Cross Volunteer of the Quarter," October–December, 1987.

CAREER
SUMMARY   OPERATORY:

• Assisted dentists in restorative, endodontic, prosthodontic, pedodontic, oral surgery, and general dentistry procedures.

• Experienced in Oral Anatomy, Physiology, Pharmacology, Bacteriology, Sterilization, and Disinfection.

• Cleaned, disinfected, and sterilized rooms, equipment, and instruments.

• Kept operatories fully stocked.

• Ordered supplies as needed.

• Maintained handpieces and equipment in accordance with manufacturers' specifications.

LABORATORY:

• Ran sterilizers (Autoclave, Chemiclave, and Kavo Klave).

• Ran instruments through disinfectants and ultrasonic cleaner.

• Poured models for biteblocks, custom trays, and ortho appliances.

• Trimmed models and made biteblocks and custom trays.

• Developed and mounted X rays.

CUSTOMERS' COMMENTS

If your work is in the area of marketing or consulting, where you have considerable contact with customers, any complimentary remarks these individuals have made to you can be used in your résumé.

Here's how Harmon Benning, a Harvard M.B.A. and consultant in the telecommunications industry, advantageously used comments made by customers while he was employed by Mobile Market Strategies and Marketing Corporation of America (only the first page of his résumé is given):

Harmon X. Benning
3675 Las Brisas
Sarasota, FL 34238
(813) 923-8333

PROFILE

An innovative marketer with a history of achievements, both in launching new businesses and in building profits and sales of established companies. Proven results in adapting consumer marketing methods and ideas to new telecommunications and computer ventures.

EXPERIENCE

MOBILE MARKET STRATEGIES, Sarasota, FL. 1991–1995.

Project Manager for this consulting firm.

- Performed marketing and strategy consulting for companies in telecommunications and information technologies. Projects provided solutions for new businesses and markets.
- Over two years, completed 7 projects for 3 divisions of BellSouth. One senior client executive stated, "Insightful . . . strong direction." Another commented, "Really good with a blank canvas."
- Designed an innovative distribution-channel strategy for division of Japanese multinational corporation.

MARKETING CORPORATION OF AMERICA, Westport, CT. 1990–1991.

Senior Consultant.

- Team Leader on projects for clients including Kraft General Foods and Quaker Oats.
- Led development of growth program for division of Kraft General Foods. Client began immediate implementation. Year 1 profits exceeded goal.
- Managed assessment and projection of key competitor's strategic behavior for division of Quaker Oats. President called project, "A home run, out of the park."

EMERGING CONSUMER PRODUCTS, INC., Milwaukee, WI. 1986–1990.

Founder and **President**.

- Launched a company to produce and market a nonsour refrigerated yogurt for supermarket distribution.
- Achieved 10% share in metro test market, generating active acquisition interest from several of the largest marketers of yogurt in the U.S. and Europe. Brand was sold to another yogurt manufacturer.
- Built a higher Nielsen share in test market than major brands of three Fortune 200 companies. Product also outperformed comparable Dannon and Yoplait products in "blind" taste tests conducted by those two companies, winning by 64-to-36 margins.

UNTRADITIONAL STATEMENTS

It's clear that there are certain procedures you need to follow in order to produce a topflight résumé; there are also particular things you must avoid. But this doesn't mean that there isn't room for creativity when writing your résumé, that you must follow a rigid formula in order to produce an excellent background summary. Nothing could be further from the truth.

It will be to your advantage if you inject some creativity into your résumé and say something that's a little different from what you're expected to. If you can make one or two statements about yourself that aren't the garden variety kind, then as you advance your candidacy by describing your strengths and accomplishments you'll also be adding individuality and flavor to your résumé.

Following are examples of two job hunters who did exactly that.

The first is Stephen Lauffer, an M.B.A. and C.P.A. with eight years' business experience.

Stephen began his discussion of his employment at The Racquets Resort by announcing that he had been hired without having had any experience at all in the resort/athletic-club industry.

This is an unusual statement to make because what you're "supposed" to convey in a résumé is how *experienced* you are in a certain area, not how *inexperienced* you are.

But what Stephen accomplished by taking this approach was to demonstrate his overall talents as a businessman. When employers learn of his achievements at The Racquets Resort, especially in such a short period of time, their estimation of him will rise, due to the fact that he had no previous experience in this business. Stephen's accomplishments were the result of pure talent and hard work. This makes him attractive to employers in all businesses, not just in the resort/athletic-club industry.

A second thing Stephen did that was out of the ordinary was to state in his discussion of his work for GE Capital Corporation that he was the only person on a 4-member team who didn't have a C.P.A. certification (see the second bulleted item). Again, he advances his capability by divulging that he was successful despite the fact that he lacked a type of training that the job traditionally required. Here's his résumé (only the first page appears):

Stephen Lauffer
81 57th Street West
Bradenton, FL 34209
(813) 792-4027

PROFILE   An M.B.A. and C.P.A. with an outstanding record of results in Financial and Business Analysis as well as Management. Have produced dramatic increases in revenues and profits. Highly imaginative and resourceful—a continuous generator of new ideas.

EXPERIENCE   THE RACQUETS RESORT, Naples, FL. 1992–1995.

Operations Manager. With no experience in the resort or athletic-club industry, analyzed operations of this 30-acre, 38-tennis-court, 50-condominium resort and effected changes to boost revenues and profits. Revamped marketing, financial systems and controls, facilities, athletic and social programs, cuisine, and personnel policies. Also hired and trained a new staff.

- Increased membership in a declining environment and generated a profitable fiscal year (1993) for the first time in 4 years for the facility's adult-tennis complex. 1994 showed 100% growth over 1993.

- Boosted on-site condominium rental income 50% from previous year. Especially successful in attracting European, Canadian, and South American travelers.

- Increased domestic Corporate and Group revenues by 30%.

BRADENTON STUDIOS, Bradenton, FL. 1991–1992.

General Manager. Launched this advertising/commercial photography business. Obtained the initial financing and wrote the business and marketing plans.

GE CAPITAL CORPORATION, RETAILER FINANCIAL SERVICES DIVISION, Atlanta, GA. 1988–1991.

Financial Analyst. Unit developed and implemented open-end (revolving) and closed-end (nonrevolving) consumer financing programs for client companies, and also provided clients with short-and long-term debt and equity financing.

- Prepared annual portfolio reviews, in excess of $1 billion, for senior management with investment authority within 16 industries. Reviewed prospective transactions ranging from $50 million to $500 million including transaction structure, business viability analysis, legal compliance and due diligence.

- Selected as member of a 4-person team that integrated Montgomery Ward Credit Corporation into GE Capital, the two entities totaling $6 billion in earning assets. Was the only person on this team without a C.P.A. certification.

- Saved GE $10 million annually through consolidating 8 back offices into 3.

The second example of a job hunter making untraditional remarks is
Sally McCullough.

Sally did three things that were unusual. First, she began her résumé
by stating in her objective the minimum amount of income that she
would accept. Second, she mentioned the number of hours she worked
at Independent Life Insurance Company. Third, she concluded the document by stating not only that she's a single mother, but that she has
three children who are six, eight, and 12 years old.

When you combine these statements, they all fit together and tell a
story: Sally is the breadwinner for the household and needs this level of
income because she has three other mouths to feed.

Sally also makes it clear that she's a hard worker, doesn't feel that
she's entitled to special treatment because of her responsibilities, and
isn't looking for a cushy job. She evidences this in two ways. First, she
states in her objective that she's seeking a commission-based sales position, not a salaried job. Second, she conveys her determination and
motivation through stating that she has performed extensive cold-calling plus door-to-door prospecting throughout her career, working as
many as 50–60 hours per week.

Sally's untraditional statements add originality, vitality, and a sense of
commitment to an already strong background. It's certain that whoever
hires her is going to get one dedicated worker. Moreover, any employers who don't have positions that can satisfy her financial goals won't
waste her time by contacting her. Sally's résumé follows:

Sally McCullough
3619 S. Lockwood Ridge Rd.
Sarasota, FL 34231
(813) 923-4984

OBJECTIVE   A commission-based sales position providing the opportunity to earn at least $40,000 the first year and $60,000 the next.

SALES
SKILLS
- An excellent qualifier and closer.
- An outgoing and convincing personality.
- Enthusiastic, persistent, and goal-driven.
- The ability to relate well with a wide variety of people.
- A high energy level with strong follow-through.

EXPERIENCE   DOMESTIC SERVICES, Sarasota, FL. 1991–present.

Founder and **Operator** of this business that cleans homes and provides house-sitting, pet-sitting, and errand services.

- Identified good neighborhoods for developing business, performed extensive door-to-door prospecting, sold service agreements, and established the initial customer base.
- Expanded business through additional cold-calling plus generation of referrals.
- Currently service 26 accounts.

INDEPENDENT LIFE INSURANCE COMPANY, Sarasota, FL. 1990–1991.

Sales Agent.

- Sold life and health insurance policies to residents in the Newtown community.
- Performed telephone prospecting and cold-calling on door-to-door basis, often selling and prospecting 50–60 hours a week.
- Consistently achieved quota. Generated a substantial number of leads and referrals.
- Traveled to clients' homes to collect premiums when overdue.

VETERINARY REFERENCE LABORATORY, Tampa, FL. 1983–1990.

Branch Manager of this company that performed diagnostic testing for veterinarians. Managed 6 people with complete responsibility for all operations.

- Increased sales from $4,000 a month in 1983 to $30,000 monthly in 1990.
- Opened up and built satellite facilities in Pinellas, Hillsborough, Pasco, Polk, Manatee, and Sarasota counties.

Sally McCullough
Page 2

- Personally performed all the marketing and sales activities. This included calling on prospective accounts, introducing company's services, and closing business.

- Due to results achieved, corporate office in Dallas, TX, adopted this satellite marketing approach and instituted it in 60 branches nationwide. Trained many Branch Managers in satellite development techniques.

IMMUNO VET, Tampa, FL. 1981–1983.

Sales/Service Representative for this veterinary research and diagnostic laboratory.

ST. FRANCIS OF ASSISI'S RETIREMENT CENTER, Tampa, FL. 1979–1981.

Dietary Assistant.

EDUCATION   Tampa Catholic High School, Tampa, FL. 1979.

PERSONAL   A single mother with 3 children, ages 6, 8, and 12.

References furnished on request.

What Sally and Steve chose to discuss about themselves are examples of the kinds of untraditional remarks that can be made to add a creative touch to a résumé. See if there's something about you—it could be an aspect of your job objective, some education or training that you lack, or an obstacle or hurdle you had to overcome—that's unique or different and that will make a positive impact on prospective employers. If you can come up with something that's new and fresh and that at the same time will add to your credibility and capability, it will make for exciting reading and produce more interviews.

PERSONAL INFORMATION

Another creative way to embellish your background is to include a personal section that sets forth information that will make a highly favorable impression on prospective employers. This section can also be used to prevent people from having a negative, stereotypical reaction to a particular type of background.

Gretchen Schmidt was a brilliant, young computer systems analyst/programmer. She wanted to move into a marketing-support position where she would play a key role in developing potential accounts and bringing in new business. This type of work necessitates a sales-oriented personality, which many people lack who perform Gretchen's highly technical work.

To ensure that no one mistakes Gretchen for a shy person with a passive personality, she included a personal section in her résumé that shows she enjoys group activities, especially ones that require active participation and a high energy level. Here's her résumé:

Gretchen Schmidt
2505 S. Ocean Ave.
Palm Beach, FL 33480
(407) 582-3806

OBJECTIVE   Systems Analysis/Design and Marketing Support in a consulting environment.

EXPERIENCE   **ACCOUNTING SOLUTIONS**, West Palm Beach, FL. January 1995–present.

Application Developer. Worked on 3 separate projects since joining this software development company.

"AMEIA," an Access-based product that provides data on administration and management of employees on international assignments. October 1995–present.

- Performed the programming, generation of reports, plus design of the user interface.

"M.T.T.P.," an application providing management tools for tax practices. March–September, 1995.

- Served as Lead Tester/Designer.
- Conferred with users on system design and functionality.
- Created test cycles for new functions.
- Performed customer telephone support.
- Served as Subject Matter Expert for documentation of product.

" Time Reports," January–March, 1995.

- Designed a Proof of Concept prototype using Excel 4.0 Macros.

COMPUTER   Microsoft Word, Excel, Excel 4.0 Macros, and Access Basic;
BACKGROUND   DOS and Quick Screen; specialized training in MS Basic and GUI Design.

EDUCATION   B.S., Business Administration, University of Florida. December 1995.
Major: Decision and Information Sciences. GPA: 3.95.
Specialization: Management Science.

Course work included Lotus 1.2.3., Quattro Pro, dBase, WordPerfect, DOS, COBOL, LISP, C, SQL, LINDO, GINO, GPSS/H, and Briefcase.

PERSONAL   Interests include Tae Kwon Do, beach volleyball, line dancing, and bicycle racing.

PRESTIGIOUS COMPANIES

Some job hunters have worked for prestigious companies and want this to be prominent on their résumé. Their belief, and often rightly so, is that other companies who are leaders in their industry prefer to hire individuals who have worked for equally successful organizations.

The way to call attention to the companies you've worked for is to set their names in boldface type while using regular-face type for your job titles (both company names and job titles will be in capital letters).

Here's how Denise Mumford constructed her résumé so that the names *Tropicana, Polaroid, First National Bank of Boston,* and *State Street Bank & Trust Company* would stand out.

Denise Mumford
50 Raymond St.
Sarasota, FL 34233
(813) 923-6297

OBJECTIVE   Credit Manager at a large industrial company.

EXPERIENCE   **TROPICANA PRODUCTS, INC.**, Bradenton, FL. 1993–1996.

KEY ACCOUNTS CREDIT ANALYST.

Complete responsibility for credit maintenance and collection activities of all accounts that purchase in excess of $1,000,000 annually.

- Ensured that accounts remained within credit limits.
- Reduced over-90-day receivables by 65%.
- Instituted new systems, procedures, and controls that increased operating efficiencies and reduced paper work by 50%.
- Performed extensive interaction with sales force in the notification and resolution of credit problems.
- Helped train new hires.
- Oversaw department in absence of Manager.

POLAROID CORPORATION, Cambridge, MA. 1989–1993.

CREDIT/COLLECTION ADMINISTRATOR.

- Made credit decisions concerning new accounts and established limits.
- Reduced over-90-day receivables by 50%.
- Developed payment schedules with accounts in arrears.
- Prepared commission-due reports and journal entries for write-offs and adjustments.

FIRST NATIONAL BANK OF BOSTON, Boston, MA. 1985–1989.

SENIOR ACCOUNTANT-GENERAL ACCOUNTING.

- Handled the fixed-asset records and the depreciation for those assets.
- Prepared the monthly public-unit deposit state reports.
- Serviced bank's investments, including GNMA, FHLMC, APM (SAM), FNMA, UST Notes and the amortization of their premiums and discounts, paydowns, sales, purchases, broker options, pledged securities, FHLB Advances and FHLB Repo's, broker reverse repurchase agreements, broker repurchase agreements, and reports to Board of Directors.
- Assisted senior management with external audits.

Denise Mumford
Page 2

STATE STREET BANK & TRUST COMPANY, Boston, MA. 1980–1985.

ACCOUNTANT II-GENERAL ACCOUNTING, 1982–1985.

- As Accounts Payable Administrator, verified that all invoices were paid and that all utility bills were accounted for.
- Analyzed fixed expenses to ensure consistency.
- Handled return-deposited items plus Canadian and foreign checks.
- Prepared the monthly Sales and Use State Tax and handled the annual 1099-MISC forms.

ACCOUNTANT I-GENERAL ACCOUNTING, 1980–1982.

- Assisted Accounts Payable Clerk with computer input and checked validity of approvals.
- Ensured that all capital improvements had been approved by Board of Directors.

EDUCATION   B.S., Accounting, Boston University, 1989.

References furnished on request.

A PROGRESSION OF INCREASINGLY RESPONSIBLE POSITIONS

Some job hunters want to highlight their titles instead of the names of their employers. This is often the case when their background shows a progression of increasingly responsible positions and they want this growth to be prominent on their résumé.

The way to make your titles stand out is to set them in boldface type while placing beneath them in regular-face type the names of your employers along with their locations and your dates of employment (titles, names of employers, locations, and dates will be in upper-and lower-case letters). The résumé of Harvey Freedman illustrates this approach.

Harvey P. Freedman
467 Tulip Dr.
Sarasota, FL 34242
(813) 349-7554

PROFILE

A Senior Financial Executive with international, multi-unit manufacturing experience. Strengths include strategic planning, MIS, acquisitions and divestitures, cost reduction, plus SEC and tax reporting. A strong background in increasing revenues and operating efficiencies while reducing expenses.

EXPERIENCE

Vice President/Chief Financial Officer.
Medex Inc., Tampa, FL. 1989–1995.

Directed 25 people with complete responsibility for all financial activities including MIS and purchasing for this manufacturer of personal and health-care products. Annual sales: $75,000,000.

- Developed strategic plans and cost-reduction programs, recommended acquisitions and divestitures, and made presentations to Board of Directors.

- Closed down a domestic manufacturing facility and moved production to Far East, saving $1,000,000 annually.

- Consolidated 4 separate business units. Developed a fully integrated computer system that served manufacturing, inventory control, standard cost, purchasing, sales-order processing, and all financial modules, saving $500,000 annually.

- Instituted regular meetings with Top Management to discuss operating funds for maximizing cash retention. Program was so successful that parent holding company adopted it for all other subsidiaries.

- Negotiated refinancing of short-and long-term debt with banks.

- During frequent, extended absences of president, reviewed and made decisions on all sales and marketing product-launch programs, working-capital allocation, and cost-reduction programs. Personally decided to move production from domestic to offshore plants.

- As member of 4-person strategic marketing task force, evaluated existing marketing plans and developed and implemented alternative strategies for increasing sales.

Vice President and Controller.
Cook Bates Co., Venice, FL. 1986–1989.

Company manufactured a line of manicure implements.

- Made acquisitions that increased sales from $17,000,000 to $38,000,000.

- Divested 2 businesses, saving $600,000 annually.

- Developed systems to determine profitability of new products and to track and control inventories.

- Managed a staff of 20.

Controller.

Chemex Corporation, West Paterson, NJ. 1979–1986.

Company manufactured specialty chemicals, with annual sales of $225,000,000.

- Directed 40 people with complete responsibility for SEC reporting, federal and state tax planning and reporting, plus preparation and issuance of annual report.
- Forecasted monthly P&L and cash flows.
- Led acquisition team in high-tech specialty chemicals. Acquired 4 companies with combined annual sales of $30,000,000.
- Appointed to Board of Directors at an unprofitable subsidiary. Turned company around and generated profits of $900,000.
- Implemented LIFO method of accounting, resulting in tax savings of $1,300,000 annually.
- Member, Senior Management Committee.

Senior Financial Analyst, 1981–1984.

Financial Analyst, 1979–1981.

EDUCATION

M.B.A., Accounting, St. Johns University, Jamaica, NY. 1979.
Major: Public Accounting.

B.S., Computer Sciences, New York Institute of Technology, New York, NY. 1977.

References furnished on request.

REPETITIVE POSITIONS

If you've performed the identical work for two or more companies in succession, you'll need to be careful about how you word your job descriptions. If you state verbatim the same responsibilities and duties for each employer, your résumé will be monotonous to read and you'll appear to be a boring and uninteresting person.

You never want to write a résumé like the following, where the same job descriptions are used for The Blake Group, Nugent & Associates, and The Gilbert Organization.

Gregory R. Halverstam
1750 Sydelle St.
Sarasota, FL 34237
(813) 953-3007

OBJECTIVE   A challenging Outside Sales position with a manufacturer or distributor of
industrial products.

EXPERIENCE   **SYSCO FOOD SERVICES OF CENTRAL FLORIDA**, Sarasota, FL.
1991–present.
District Sales Representative for this broad-line distributor of food products.

- Sell $2,000,000 of meats, poultry, seafood, frozen foods, produce, and paper
  goods to chain and independent restaurants and hotels, retirement homes,
  nursing homes, and hospitals in the Bradenton, Sarasota, Venice market.
- Established 100% of accounts through cold-calling and generation of referrals.
- Make sales presentations on a one-to-one basis and to groups of up to 5
  people.

THE BLAKE GROUP, San Francisco, CA. 1989–1991.
Placement Counselor at this employment agency specializing in sales
positions.

- Interviewed individuals seeking sales positions and determined their level of
  capability and area of interest.
- Called prospective employers on phone, presented qualifications of applicants,
  and set up interviews.
- Rewrote résumés as needed for mailing to prospective employers.
- Followed up on interviews, both with employer and applicant, to facilitate a hire.
- Also performed recruitment activities for clients: searched for specific
  backgrounds according to employers' needs.

NUGENT & ASSOCIATES, Los Angeles, CA. 1987–1989.
Placement Counselor at this employment agency specializing in sales
positions.

- Interviewed individuals seeking sales positions and determined their level of
  capability and area of interest.
- Called prospective employers on phone, presented qualifications of applicants,
  and set up interviews.
- Rewrote résumés as needed for mailing to prospective employers.
- Followed up on interviews, both with employer and applicant, to facilitate a hire.
- Also performed recruitment activities for clients: searched for specific
  backgrounds according to employers' needs.

THE GILBERT ORGANIZATION, San Francisco, CA. 1985–1987.

Placement Counselor at this employment agency specializing in sales positions.

- Interviewed individuals seeking sales positions and determined their level of capability and area of interest.
- Called prospective employers on phone, presented qualifications of applicants, and set up interviews.
- Rewrote résumés as needed for mailing to prospective employers.
- Followed up on interviews, both with employer and applicant, to facilitate a hire.
- Also performed recruitment activities for clients: searched for specific backgrounds according to employers' needs.

ROYAL CROWN COLA, San Francisco, CA. 1982–1985.

Sales Representative.

- Performed extensive prospecting in the sale of carbonated beverages and presentation of promotional programs.
- Called on grocery, drug, liquor, and convenience stores.
- Serviced 30 accounts per day.

EDUCATION University of San Francisco, 1980–1982.
Studied Marketing and Business Administration.

References furnished on request.

The way to handle a succession of repetitive positions is to group the employers together and then present responsibilities and duties all at once, as follows:

THE BLAKE GROUP, San Francisco, CA. 1989–1991.
NUGENT & ASSOCIATES, Los Angeles, CA. 1987–1989.
THE GILBERT ORGANIZATION, San Francisco, CA. 1985–1987.

Placement Counselor at these employment agencies that specialized in sales positions.

- Interviewed individuals seeking sales positions and determined their level of capability and type of sales job desired.

- Called prospective employers on phone, presented qualifications of applicants, and set up interviews.

- Rewrote résumés as needed for mailing to prospective employers.

- Followed up on interviews, both with employer and applicant, to facilitate a hire.

- Also performed recruitment activities for clients: searched for specific backgrounds according to employers' needs.

Some job hunters try to eliminate repetitive job descriptions by presenting the last employment experience and then stating after the names of the previous employers "Duties same as above." This is no more effective than repeating responsibilities and duties verbatim.

In the event that you've done the same kind of work for *every employer you've ever had* (this is often the case with people working in the trades), the way to eliminate the problem of repetition is to write a functional résumé.

Grouping your employers together and then describing the work that you performed is also an effective way to conceal gaps in employment. For example, suppose that Gregory Halverstam worked for The Blake Group from 1990–1991, for Nugent & Associates from 1987–1988, and for The Gilbert Organization in 1985. He was unemployed for all of 1989 and 1986. To mask these gaps in employment, Gregory would describe his years in the personnel field as follows:

THE BLAKE GROUP, San Francisco, CA.
NUGENT & ASSOCIATES, Los Angeles, CA.
THE GILBERT ORGANIZATION, San Francisco, CA.

Placement Counselor at these employment agencies from 1985–1991. Firms specialized in sales positions.

- Interviewed individuals seeking sales positions and determined their level of capability and type of sales job desired.

- Called prospective employers on phone, presented qualifications of applicants, and set up interviews.

- Rewrote résumés as needed for mailing to prospective employers.

- Followed up on interviews, both with employer and applicant, to facilitate a hire.
- Also performed recruitment activities for clients: searched for specific backgrounds according to employers' needs.

SPECIAL JOB HUNTERS

THE CAREER CHANGER

Today, Americans are trying to change careers at a robust pace. Many people feel that the work they've been performing for so many years is no longer challenging and exciting, and they want to do something that will be more fulfilling and give greater meaning to their life. Others change careers for monetary reasons. They want to lead a lifestyle that they haven't been able to afford to date and seek work that will make this new way of life possible.

Regardless of the motivation for changing careers, here are steps to take with your résumé to enhance your qualifications.

WHEN TO HIGHLIGHT YOUR EDUCATION AND NOT YOUR WORK EXPERIENCE

If the work you want to perform *requires a special degree or certificate and you just completed your studies,* discuss your related education right after stating your job objective. The likelihood is that your recent educational training is far more important than your work experience.

When discussing your work experience, you also don't need to use bullets to draw attention to your key responsibilities, duties, and accomplishments. In fact, it's recommended that you omit these marks. There's no reason to highlight work you've done that's unrelated to your new area of interest. Describe your various contributions in a single paragraph.

Additionally, consolidate a good deal of your work experience, giving only an overview of your activities. The résumé of Claudia Rasmussen illustrates these points.

Claudia Rasmussen
72 Glen Drive
Sarasota, FL 34231
(813) 966-7650

OBJECTIVE   Massage Therapist, incorporating a holistic approach to wellness.

EDUCATION   Diploma, Sarasota School of Massage Therapy, Sarasota, FL. 1995.

- Maintained an "A" average.
- Certified Reiki Practitioner.
- 100 hours of Shiatsu Training.
- Will be Nationally Certified and Licensed in Florida, January 1996.

Masters Degree in Education, Lynchburg College, Lynchburg, VA. 1974.
GPA: 3.70.

B.A., Economics, Randolph Macon Woman's College, Lynchburg, VA.
1973.
Minor: Humanities.

EXPERIENCE   TEACHING: 1988–1994 and 1974–1983.

Teacher. Instructed 1st–6th grade students at public and private schools,
plus tutored 2nd–8th grade students and adults. Subjects included
elementary-school basics and remedial reading for students with learning
disabilities. Supervised after-school activity clubs, designed and
implemented testing procedures and student evaluation programs, and
wrote and produced plays.

Also held positions of **Team Leader**, responsible for weekly meetings with
Administration and then disseminating information to faculty members,
and **Faculty Advisor**, responsible for monthly meetings with District
Administration and imparting information to entire faculty and school
administration.

Employers consisted of Pinellas Park Elementary School, Pinellas Park,
FL; Sylvan Learning Center, St. Petersburg, FL; Limetree Academy
Christiansted, U.S. Virgin Islands; Alexander Henderson School, U.S.
Virgin Islands; Rustburg Middle School, Rustburg, VA; T.C. Miller School,
Lynchburg, VA; and Phenix Elementary School, Phenix, VA.

TRAVEL INDUSTRY: 1983–1988.

Travel Agent with Thomas Cook Travel Agency, Basking Ridge, NJ.

Responsible for reservations and data entry on SABRE computers.

Customer Service Manager/Flight Attendant with People Express
Airlines, Newark, NJ.

Managed ground operations, performed computer reservations and
scheduling, and assisted customers while in flight.

WHEN TO HIGHLIGHT YOUR KEY SKILLS AND STRENGTHS

If you're changing careers and the work you want to do *doesn't require a degree or certificate in a particular field*, then it's essential to highlight those skills and strengths that will show that you have the ability to perform this work. You need to do this for three reasons.

First, your educational training won't help you get interviews. This is because the position you're seeking doesn't require schooling in a specific area.

Second, prospective employers won't be that impressed by your accomplishments, due to the fact that the tasks you've performed throughout your career will be quite different from those that you'll be responsible for at your new position.

Third, if you're thinking that because skills can be transferrable from one position to another that prospective employers will read your résumé, analyze your background, then determine what skills you used in order to decide if you have the right qualifications for the job you want, don't count on this happening. Interviewers won't go through your work history with a fine-tooth comb to figure out what your underlying abilities are. You must do this analytical work for them and prominently state your skills on your résumé.

The best way to do this is to create a section titled "Related Strengths" or "Related Skills" and describe your key talents here. Place this section right after your job objective. Here's the résumé of George Forte. George wants to become a flight attendant with an airline and has no experience doing this type of work. Notice how he used a "Related Strengths" section at the outset of his résumé to call attention to his most important assets.

George Forte
1782 Wisteria St.
Sarasota, FL 34239
(813) 953-3281

OBJECTIVE   Flight Attendant.

RELATED   • A world traveler with excellent communication skills and an
STRENGTHS   outgoing personality.

                  • Bilingual in English and Italian; understand spoken French.

                  • Relate well with a wide variety of people.

                  • A quick thinker who remains calm under pressure.

                  • Work effectively in tight schedules.

                  • Well-organized and attentive to detail.

EDUCATION   University of Florence, Florence, Italy. 1990–1992.
                  Studied Political Science and Journalism.

                  University of Rome, Rome, Italy. 1988–1990.
                  Studied Italian, Political Science, and History.

                  Diploma, Sarasota High School, Sarasota, FL. 1988.

EXPERIENCE   **COLONY BEACH & TENNIS RESORT**, Longboat Key, FL.
                  1994–present.

                  Front Desk Clerk. Check in and check out guests. Post guests' charges
                  and track and monitor their payments. Manage a $1,000 cash bank.
                  Responsible for responding to all emergency situations and calls.

                  FROGGY'S RESTAURANT, Sarasota, FL. 1993–1994.

                  Assistant to Owner. Scheduled hours for 6–10 employees. Ordered food,
                  beverages, and supplies. Responsible for upkeep and security. Performed
                  cashiering.

                  TUTTO RADIO, 95.7 FM, Florence, Italy. 1992–1993.

                  DJ/Reporter/Marketing Assistant. Reported news, interviewed
                  celebrities, served as disc jockey, and sold air time.

                  References furnished on request.

WHEN TO HIGHLIGHT VOLUNTEER AND COMMUNITY ACTIVITIES

Some career changers are seeking work that's an extension of the activities they've been performing on a volunteer basis—such as work they've done for community organizations—and their goal has nothing to do with the duties they've been performing for their employer. In this instance, these volunteer activities should appear at the beginning of a résumé. What's more, it need not be stated that this work was done on a volunteer basis. This can be explained during the interview.

Look at the first résumé of Felicity Dalton. She appears to be unqualified for a position in the field of special events or public relations—which is her job objective—because her résumé describes no experience in this area. Her background is in retailing. However, in Felicity's second résumé, she elaborates on the volunteer work she did for numerous community organizations—under "Special Events/Public Relations Experience"—and it becomes clear that she is accomplished in both of these fields.

Just because someone did work on a volunteer basis and didn't get paid for their contributions doesn't mean that they're not proficient in this activity or that this experience doesn't belong in their résumé. If volunteer work is pertinent to a job objective, it should be included in the document. Often, in fact, it will be the crux of the experience that's being described. This is the case in Felicity's second résumé.

(Notice that in the "Special Events/Public Relations Experience" section, Felicity didn't give the names of the organizations she worked for, similar to when using the functional format. Also notice that in the "Retail Experience" section, she followed the traditional chronological-format approach of giving employers' names, locations, and dates of employment.)

Felicity Dalton
13 Palmer Ave.
Sarasota, FL 34239
(813) 953-9504

OBJECTIVE   Special Events Coordinator or Public Relations Specialist.

EXPERIENCE   **FAY AND JUDY'S**, Sarasota, FL. 1990–present.

Co-Owner and **Manager** of this retailer of women's leather accessories. Complete responsibility for all operations including sales, buying, customer service, merchandising, display and floor planning, inventory and expense control, and upkeep.

- Opened this store with partner and recruited, hired, and trained all personnel, including 1 Sales Supervisor and 2 Sales Associates.

- Generated sales in the last 12 months that were 20% greater than previous year.

- Educate staff on products and train personnel in sales techniques.

- Inform staff of advertising and promotional campaigns and orient them on new products.

- Perform weekly and monthly sales analyses.

- Personally sell merchandise as time permits.

ETIENNE AIGNER, Orlando, FL. 1989–1990.

Assistant Manager at this retailer of women's accessories.

- Managed 10 Sales Associates.

- Assisted Manager with all store operations.

- Sold merchandise and consistently exceeded quota.

CASUAL CORNER, Orlando, FL. 1988–1989.

Lead Sales Associate for this retailer of women's fashions.

- Consistently exceeded quota.

- Helped train and motivate other Sales Associates.

- Assisted Manager in merchandising, displays, cash control, and store upkeep.

Felicity Dalton
Page 2

SHOES, SHOES, SHOES, Orlando, FL. 1987–1988.

Sales Associate at this women's shoe store.

- #1 Sales Associate on the floor.
- Received and tagged merchandise and assisted with merchandising and displays.

COMMUNITY
ORGANIZATIONS
Ringling Museum of Art.
Gulf Coast Heritage Association.
American Heart Association.
Sarasota Memorial Hospital.
Ringling School of Art & Design.
Asolo Performing Arts Center.
Junior League of Sarasota.
The Players Theater.

EDUCATION
B.A., Marketing, University of South Florida. 1987.

References furnished on request.

Felicity Dalton
13 Palmer Ave.
Sarasota, FL 34239
(813) 953-9504

OBJECTIVE

Special Events Coordinator or Public Relations Specialist.

SPECIAL EVENTS/PUBLIC RELATIONS EXPERIENCE

- Since 1990, have been creating, developing, and implementing marketing strategies and fund-raisers for organizations including hospitals, colleges, performing arts centers, performing arts groups, charities, and museums. Events have included patrons' parties, polo matches, music fests, street fairs, balls and dances, runs, and picnics.

- Plan agendas for events, negotiate for and obtain sites, and hire and supervise required personnel and subcontractors.

- Develop publicity, compose program books, and sell advertising space.

- Generate revenues of up to $90,000 per event.

- Work closely with media representatives, public relations firms, and advertising agencies in coordinating the creation of ads, press releases, and placements. Personally write copy and design ads.

RETAIL EXPERIENCE

FAY AND JUDY'S, Sarasota, FL. 1990–present.

Co-Owner and **Manager** of this retailer of women's leather accessories. Complete responsibility for all operations including sales, buying, customer service, merchandising, display and floor planning, inventory and expense control, and upkeep.

- Opened this store with partner and recruited, hired, and trained all personnel, including 1 Sales Supervisor and 2 Sales Associates.

- Generated sales in the last 12 months that were 20% greater than previous year.

- Educate staff on products and train personnel in sales techniques.

- Inform staff of advertising and promotional campaigns and orient them on new products.

- Perform weekly and monthly sales analyses.

- Personally sell merchandise as time permits.

ETIENNE AIGNER, Orlando, FL. 1989–1990.

Assistant Manager at this retailer of women's accessories.

- Managed 10 Sales Associates.

- Assisted Manager with all store operations.

- Sold merchandise and consistently exceeded quota.

CASUAL CORNER, Orlando, FL. 1988–1989.

Lead Sales Associate for this retailer of women's fashions.

- Consistently exceeded quota.

- Helped train and motivate other Sales Associates.

- Assisted Manager in merchandising, displays, cash control, and store upkeep.

SHOES, SHOES, SHOES, Orlando, FL. 1987–1988.

Sales Associate at this women's shoe store.

- #1 Sales Associate on the floor.

- Received and tagged merchandise and assisted with merchandising and displays.

COMMUNITY ORGANIZATIONS

Ringling Museum of Art.

Gulf Coast Heritage Association.

American Heart Association.

Sarasota Memorial Hospital.

Ringling School of Art & Design.

Asolo Performing Arts Center.

Junior League of Sarasota.

The Players Theater.

EDUCATION

B.A., Marketing, University of South Florida. 1987.

References furnished on request.

Career Change and Concealing Your Age

If you've made a career change, you'll be able to conceal your age in the event that you believe it will be advantageous to appear younger in your résumé than you really are.

The reason you'll be able to do this is that you're not obligated to discuss any work experience prior to the time you entered your current field. Remember, your résumé is only a summary of your capability as it relates to the type of position you're seeking; it's not your life story.

You'll be able to cover up your age, however, only if you don't have a college degree. In this instance, it isn't necessary to state the years you attended college since you didn't graduate. If you do have a degree, then your date of graduation will give away your age, assuming you completed your studies four years after finishing high school, like most people do.

Never try to hide your age by omitting your date of graduation. Employers could become suspicious about the absence of this date and assume that you're older than you really are.

The résumé of Chuck Merriman is a good example of how a career change can be effective for concealing age.

Chuck is 47 years old and was employed by the County of Sarasota, Florida, from 1969 to 1979. During this 10-year period, he audited financial reports for guardianship and child-support cases.

In 1979, Chuck decided that he was tired of a desk job and was also discouraged by the lack of opportunity for advancement without having a college degree. He wanted to make use of his hobby, carpentry, and he went into the construction business.

Here's Chuck's résumé, 17 years later, where he appears to be 37 because he omitted from the document the 10 years he spent with the County of Sarasota, Florida, auditing financial reports. This experience had nothing to do with his current line of work, so there was no reason to include it in his background. He began his résumé when he entered the construction business.

Chuck Merriman
17 Pond Lane
Sarasota, FL 34233
(813) 922-6086

OBJECTIVE   A Construction Management position with a growing company specializing in commercial properties.

EXPERIENCE   **THE GREER GROUP**, Bradenton, FL. 1991–present.

Superintendent of Maintenance, Southwark Plaza.

- Manage a crew of 18 in maintaining 1 occupied high-rise, 2 high-rises under construction, and a 15-acre site with 188 low-rise town houses.

- Increased work output by 30%.

- Introduced MAPS gas, which significantly decreased labor and soldering costs.

- Trained 3 people who were quickly promoted to supervisory positions.

- Initially joined company as **Superintendent of Plumbing & Welding**.

JOHN E. BOYD CONSTRUCTION, INC., Miami, FL. 1990–1991.

Construction Superintendent-Commercial.

- Built a 10,000-square-foot warehouse.

- Constructed additions plus the renovation of a 150,000-square-foot manufacturing facility.

- Performed computerized scheduling on TIME-LINE SOFTWARE.

PENNMARK CONSTRUCTION COMPANY, Orlando, FL. 1985–1990.

Field Superintendent, with multisite responsibility.

- Performed new construction plus the renovation of 5 shopping malls.

- Built the Drug Emporium, Rocking Horse Child Care Center, U.S. Toy, West Coast Video, plus other facilities.

POINT STREET PARTNERS, Philadelphia, PA. 1982–1985.

Project Manager.

- Rehabbed over 300 houses and apartment buildings in Pennsylvania and New Jersey.

Chuck Merriman
Page 2

DELLA CONSTRUCTION COMPANY, Willingboro, NJ. 1979–1982.
Carpenter/Foreman.

- Ran a small crew doing residential and commercial renovations and additions.

EDUCATION   Temple University, Philadelphia, PA.
Studied Accounting and Business Administration for 2 years.

References furnished on request.

THE "PARTIAL" CAREER CHANGER

Some job hunters aren't trying to change careers as much as they're desiring to do the same type of work they once performed in the past, say five or ten years ago. In this instance, the best way to present a background is through a modified version of the chronological résumé.

Jerry Kimura is such a job hunter. After having held two different positions over a 12-year period of time, Jerry wanted to get back into the business of selling home-entertainment products, i.e., stereo systems, video systems and accessories, and televisions. Here's his original résumé, before modifications:

Jerry Kimura
3627 Countryside Way
Sarasota, FL 34233
(813) 921-8505

OBJECTIVE

A challenging commission-based sales position with a retailer of home-entertainment products, with the goal of growing into a management responsibility.

EXPERIENCE

SARASOTA CHEVROLET, INC., Sarasota, FL. 1995–present.

Sales Consultant at this Chevrolet dealership.

- Sell new and used cars and trucks. Also lease vehicles.
- Qualify prospects to determine level of buying interest, features desired, and price ceiling.
- Follow up on prospects via telephone to close business.
- Actively work customer list to generate referrals.

KIMURA PHOTO CENTER, Key West, FL. 1984–1995.

Owner/Operator of this photographic studio.

- Took photographs for weddings, special events, PR/brochures, catalogs, high school seniors, passport/ID, modeling portfolios, as well as boudoir/glamour, aerial, and architectural needs.
- Provided the services of developing, enlargements, reproductions, prints from slides, and display transparencies.

OVERSEAS ELECTRONICS/NATIONWIDE VIDEO DISTRIBUTORS, INC., Miami, FL. 1980–1984.

General Sales Manager for this mail-order company and exporter of stereo systems, video products and accessories, and televisions. Company was the largest distributor of videotape products in the Southeastern United States.

- One of the 4 initial employees that grew company from a zero sales base into a $12,000,000 a year business.
- Defined the product line, located vendors, and did the purchasing. Key suppliers included Sony, TDK, Panasonic, BASF, RCA, Hitachi, and JVC.
- Developed commission schedule for the sales force and hired, trained, and supervised 18 mail-order sales reps plus 6 reps for the storefront operation.
- Coordinated advertising programs with agency and directed production of the quarterly catalog.
- Represented company at all trade shows.

BRAND ELECTRONICS, INC., Miami, FL. 1977–1980.

Store Manager at this 8-unit chain that sold stereo systems, video products, and televisions.

- Managed 3 different stores, each a promotion. Hired, trained, scheduled, supervised, and motivated up to 12 sales personnel at a unit.
- As Manager of the South Miami store, achieved highest sales level in unit's history.
- Transferred to an underperforming unit and retrained sales force. Built store to #2 in profits in chain.
- Promoted to Manager of Warehouse Outlet, the highest volume unit in the system.
- Store responsibilities also included Marketing, Merchandising, and P&L statements.

Initially joined company as a Sales Associate. Due to outstanding sales production, quickly promoted to Store Manager.

BURDINES DEPARTMENT STORES, Miami, FL. 1975–1977.

Salesperson.

- Sold stereos and advanced consumer electronics while attending college.
- Consistently #1 salesperson in the department.

EDUCATION

Miami-Dade Community College, South Miami, FL. 1976–1977.
Studied Chemistry.

University of Miami, Coral Gables, FL. 1973–1976.
Studied Music and Art.

References furnished on request.

As you can see, the problem with this résumé is it shows that Jerry has sold cars and operated a photography studio since 1984, work that has nothing to do with selling home-entertainment products. His experience prior to this, however, is picture-perfect for his objective; he's had three excellent employment experiences in the home-entertainment field.

Accordingly, Jerry modifies his chronological resume as follows:

1. He changes the "Experience" heading to read "Home-Entertainment Sales/Sales Management Experience." This accomplishes two things. First, the heading now directly relates to Jerry's job objective. Second, this heading allows Jerry to present only his home-entertainment background and omit all discussion about his selling cars and having operated a photography studio, work that's unrelated to his objective.

2. He omits dates of employment (there's no reason to state that he's beginning his résumé with experience that's 11 years old) and describes the home-entertainment background in the order in which it will make the most favorable impression on interviewers: first, Brand Electronics; next, Overseas Electronics/Nationwide Video Distributors; and last, Burdines.

3. He gives a brief description of each employer before listing his titles and describing his contributions.

4. He adds an "Employment History" section to account for the last 11 years of his work experience and to provide dates of employment.

Here's Jerry's modified chronological resume:

Jerry Kimura
3627 Country Place Blvd.
Sarasota, FL 34233
(813) 921-8505

OBJECTIVE

A challenging commission-based sales position with a retailer of home-entertainment products, with the goal of growing into a management responsibility.

HOME-ENTERTAINMENT SALES/SALES MANAGEMENT EXPERIENCE

BRAND ELECTRONICS, INC.-An 8-unit chain selling stereo systems, video products, and televisions.

Store Manager.

- Managed 3 different stores, each a promotion. Hired, trained, scheduled, supervised, and motivated up to 12 sales personnel at a unit.
- As Manager of the South Miami store, achieved highest sales level in unit's history.
- Transferred to an underperforming unit and retrained sales force. Built store to #2 in profits in chain.
- Promoted to Manager of Warehouse Outlet, the highest volume unit in the system.
- Store responsibilities also included Marketing, Merchandising, and P&L statements.
- Initially joined company as a Sales Associate. Due to outstanding sales production, quickly promoted to Store Manager.

OVERSEAS ELECTRONICS/NATIONWIDE VIDEO DISTRIBUTORS, INC.-A mail-order company and exporter of stereo systems, video products and accessories, and televisions. Company was the largest distributor of videotape products in the Southeastern United States.

General Sales Manager.

- One of the 4 initial employees that grew this company from a zero sales base into a $12,000,000 a year business.
- Defined the product line, located vendors, and did the purchasing. Key suppliers included Sony, TDK, Panasonic, BASF, RCA, Hitachi, and JVC.
- Developed commission schedule for the sales force and hired, trained, and supervised 18 mail-order sales reps plus 6 reps for the storefront.
- Coordinated advertising programs with agency and directed production of the quarterly catalog.
- Represented company at all trade shows.

Jerry Kimura
Page 2

BURDINES DEPARTMENT STORES
Salesperson.

- Sold stereos and advanced consumer electronics while attending college.
- Consistently #1 salesperson in the department.

EDUCATION

Miami-Dade Community College, South Miami, FL. 1976–1977.
Studied Chemistry.

University of Miami, Coral Gables, FL. 1973–1976.
Studied Music and Art.

EMPLOYMENT HISTORY

Sarasota Chevrolet, Inc., Sarasota, FL. 1995–present. Sales Consultant.
Kimura Photo Center, Key West, FL. 1984–1995. Owner/Operator.
Overseas Electronics/Nationwide Video Distributors, Inc., Miami, FL. 1980–1984.
   General Sales Manager.
Brand Electronics, Inc., Miami, FL. 1977–1980. Store Manager.
Burdines Department Stores, Miami, FL. 1975–1977. Salesperson.

References furnished on request.

THE GRADUATING STUDENT

Graduating students are hired more for their potential than they are for the immediate contribution they'll make. If you've just completed your studies, or are about to, there are four ways to convey your potential in your resume:

1. through listing the courses you've taken;
2. by stating your G.P.A. if it was 3.50 or higher;
3. through describing your extracurricular activities; and
4. by stating part-time work you did while at school, part- or full-time positions you held during the summer, and the amount of your education that you paid for.

When presenting your educational background, list the key courses you've taken that pertain to the field you want to enter. This will convey your ability to perform the type of work you're seeking. In the event that your studies don't directly relate to this work, don't list your course material. Just state your major.

Employers consider participation in extracurricular activities to be a good indicator of important factors such as having a genuine interest in the field of study (when these activities are directly related to the major being pursued), being a joiner versus a loner, having the ability to work with others in a team capacity, and, often, having leadership qualities. If you participated in extracurricular activities, be sure to list them.

Employers are also extremely impressed with applicants who worked during their college years to help pay for their education. They consider this to demonstrate motivation, a high energy-level, plus maturity (this doesn't mean, of course, that students who didn't work their way through college don't possess these qualities). Many employers, in fact, place more emphasis on someone's having worked to pay for their education than they do on having achieved high grades or having participated in important extracurricular activities. Always discuss jobs you held while at college—regardless of the type of work you did and whether or not it was related to your major—and state the portion of your education that you paid for.

Here are examples of how three different graduating students described their course material, extracurricular activities, and work experience in their résumé:

Anthony O. Mignone
10915 Bristol Bay Dr., #214
Bradenton, FL 34209
(813) 798-5041

OBJECTIVE

A challenging entry-level position that will utilize my background in mathematics and statistics.

EDUCATION

B.S., Mathematics/Statistics, University of Connecticut, 1995.

Course work included:

Analytical Statistics	Non-Parametric Equations
Actuarial Math	Probability
Theory of Interest	Linear Algebra
Numerical Analysis	Statistical Probability I & II
Statistical Engineering	Basic Calculus I–IV
	Introduction to Statistics

COMPUTER SKILLS

Hardware: PCs and IBM mainframes.
Software: SASS and WordPerfect 5.1.

STRENGTHS

- Outstanding numerical and analytical skills.
- Attentive to detail.
- Well organized with excellent follow-through.
- A quick learner.

References furnished on request.

Carl T. Giddings
83 Easton Street
Sarasota, FL 34238
(813) 925-9832

OBJECTIVE

Position as Clinical Social Worker in a Hospital or Psychiatric Hospital. Long-term goal is to be a Psychotherapist in Private Practice.

EDUCATION

M.A., Counseling Psychology, University of West Florida, 1995.
    Thesis: "Hypoactive Sexual Desire Disorder." G.P.A. 3.72.

Courses included:

- Theory of Personality
- Theory of Individual Counseling
- Group Counseling
- Psychopathology
- Psychiatric Psychopathology

- Advanced Behavior Modification
- Marital & Family Therapy
- Human Sexuality
- Sex Therapy
- Research Design

B.A., Psychology, University of West Florida, 1993.

G.P.A. 3.60.

Worked throughout college and paid for 100% of educational expenses.

STRENGTHS

- Excellent analytical and evaluative skills.
- Perceptive, patient, and understanding.
- An excellent listener and communicator.
- Relate well with a wide variety of people.
- A quick thinker.

WORK EXPERIENCE

FOGARTY'S, Pensacola, FL. 1989–1995.

Sales Associate at this retailer of men's clothing and accessories. Worked part-time during the school year and full-time over the summer.

- Sold clothing and accessories.
- Performed merchandising and inventory control.
- Created displays and wrote copy for advertisements.

Additional part-time jobs included waiting on tables, painting houses, and construction work.

Heather Van Alystyne
4765 Winslow Beacon
Sarasota, FL 34235
(813) 378-3866

OBJECTIVE

A challenging Public Relations position with a growing PR Firm.

EDUCATION

B.A., Speech Communication, Indiana University. 1995.

GPA: 3.50.

EXTRACURRICULAR ACTIVITIES

- "Little 500 Hostess." Selected by Indiana University to host national corporate and private sponsors for Little 500 Bicycle Race.

- Chosen by Indiana University to assist in recruitment of prospective students as well as alumni activities and relations.

- Elected Chairman of Parent's Day. Planned and supervised the first All-Campus Reception.

- Introduced and promoted "World's Greatest College Weekend" to state and local media.

- Planned, promoted, and conducted 2 campus-wide running events as scholarship fund-raisers.

- Member of Convention Steering Comittee. Created and directed a national inter-collegiate athletic board convention. Established the program for a 3-day event.

- Elected Red Carpet Days Representative. Acquainted students and parents with campus life.

- Elected Public Relations Officer for Kappa Kappa Gamma sorority.

- Member, Debate Club.

INTERESTS

Tennis, swimming, reading, and music.

References furnished on request.

THE HOUSEWIFE REENTERING THE WORK FORCE

Just as an enormous number of people are changing careers, a great many housewives are leaving the home and going back to work.

Several factors account for this exodus from domestic life. They include:

1. the fact that children have grown up and are now independent;
2. the desire to become involved in a new activity that's challenging and stimulating;
3. the need to help out with family finances due to the rising cost of living; and
4. divorce, where there's no longer a husband to provide the financial support that's needed.

Whatever the reason may be for returning to work, many women face a common problem: they haven't been on a company's payroll for a long time and there's a huge gap in their employment history. Their fear is that their résumé will read as if they "haven't done anything" for a decade or two.

The fact of the matter is that almost all housewives have performed valuable and productive work while carrying out their daily domestic responsibilities. Granted, in many cases they weren't paid for their contributions—they often did community work on a volunteer basis—but that doesn't matter. It was important work, and describing the activities they performed will eliminate the gap in employment and lend continuity to a work history.

To illustrate how to handle this situation, let's look at the background and résumé of Margo Hover.

Margo hasn't been on a company's payroll since 1985. Born and educated in the Philippines, she received her B.S. degree in business administration in 1973 and worked for the Philippine Government from 1974–1977. In 1977 Margo joined Anacomp as a programmer/analyst. She stayed with the company until 1985, when she left to become a mother and housewife. Eleven years later, after having reared two children, Margo wants to reenter the work force. Her goal is to work once again as a programmer/analyst.

Margo's challenge in her résumé is to show her qualifications to be a programmer/analyst while also accounting for her time since 1985. Here's how she does this.

Margo selects the functional format and cites her objective, which includes information on her related work experience. This is followed by a summary of her technical skills and her background as a programmer/analyst.

Then Margo creates a section titled "Independent Projects," in which she describes her various activities since she left Anacomp.

This is followed by sections that discuss her work experience with the Philippine Government, her educational background, and her work history.

Here's Margo's résumé:

Margo Hover
326 Meadowland Circle
Sarasota, FL 34233
(813) 379-4209

OBJECTIVE

Position as Programmer/Analyst, on a contract or permanent basis. Seeking to utilize 7 years' experience in development work, direct client contact, and installation of software at client sites.

TECHNICAL SKILLS

Hardware: Various NCR mainframes, PCs, ATMs, and teller terminals.

Software: COBOL; Neat/3 - levels 1, 2; Neat/VS; Excel; Windows; 'C'; DOS; ADA.

PROGRAMMER/ANALYST EXPERIENCE

ANACOMP, INC., Sarasota, FL.

- Member of development team for CI/RF On-Line Integrated Banking Software. Clients included National Bank of Kuwait; Riyadh Bank, Saudi Arabia; Monidata, New Guinea; Republic Bank of Trinidad; and SBSA Bank, Australia.

- Performed the programming, testing, documentation, and some design of application modules.

- Conducted on-site installation of the CI/RF banking system at National Bank of Kuwait. Responsible for the English and Arabic statements, miscellaneous reports, and input processing.

- Responsible for the input and report programs for the development of an integrated Commercial Loans system for CI/RF.

- Upgraded the CI/RF Mortgage Loans from COBOL 68 to COBOL 74.

- Performed programming for the development of a foreign exchange system.

INDEPENDENT PROJECTS

- Designed, developed, and tested a screen generator for Software Development Corporation, Ft. Lauderdale, FL.

- Trained students in the use of computers at the Pine View School Media Center, Sarasota, FL.

- Assisted Sarasota elementary-school teachers in classroom activities.

- Member of Cultural Arts and Programs Committee at Pine View School, to bring in cultural and scientific programs for the students.

- Cochairperson of committee arranging special events for teachers.

MUNICIPAL/ADMINISTRATIVE EXPERIENCE

- Evaluated budget proposals for Philippine government agencies.
- Formulated organizational design of new government agencies.
- Prepared monthly statistical reports.

EDUCATION

B.S., Business Administration, University of the Philippines, 1973.

Various technical courses at Rochester Institute of Technology, Manatee Community College, and Sarasota County Technical Institute.

WORK HISTORY

Independent Projects, Sarasota, FL. 1985–present.
Anacomp, Inc., Sarasota, FL. 1978–1985.
Budget Commission, Manila, Philippines. 1976–1977.
Social Security System, Manila, Philippines. 1974–1975.

References furnished on request.

CHAPTER 6

COVER LETTERS

Once you begin your job search and are working on setting up interviews, you'll undoubtedly be mailing copies of your résumé to many people. They will include prospective employers, recruiting firms, and individuals who will be helping you with your job search in a networking capacity. A cover letter should accompany each résumé you send out.

There are three purposes to this letter: (1) to explain why you're writing the person; (2) to provide important information that will gain the reader's interest and prompt him to read your résumé; and (3) to offer information that hasn't been included in your résumé. For example, when answering an ad, you might want to add something about your background that was asked for in the ad but doesn't appear in your résumé. Or you may wish to explain why you're especially interested in interviewing with the company you're writing. Another possibility is to offer specific reasons why you feel this organization would benefit from hiring you.

A cover letter also enables you to give prospective employers an idea of the person and personality behind the résumé through the way you express yourself in your letter. While a résumé is a rather formal, structured document, a cover letter allows for individuality and freedom of expression.

You'll need a cover letter for four different situations: (1) sending your résumé to companies on an unsolicited basis, (2) responding to newspaper ads, (3) contacting recruiting firms, and (4) writing to people who may be able to help you in your job search by giving you valuable information or by introducing you to others, either for job interviews or for obtaining further information. This, of course, is called networking.

187

COVER LETTER FOR AN UNSOLICITED RÉSUMÉ

When sending your résumé to a company on an unsolicited basis, you want to write, by name and title, to the person who has the authority to hire you, not to the personnel department. If you feel that your background is so strong that you might be a threat to this individual, then write to the person at the next level up.

There's one instance when it's preferable to write to the personnel department. This is when someone is seeking an administrative or support-type position that could exist in any area in the company. A member of the personnel department will know where all of the openings are in the organization and will be able to provide the exposure that's needed.

To get the names and titles of the individuals to write to, either call the companies you're interested in or go to your local library. The reference librarian will show you the directories that list companies along with the names of their key employees.

COMPOSING THE COVER LETTER

Your letter should be written on personal letterhead that omits a business phone number.

Begin your letter by writing "Dear Mr.————:" or "Dear Ms.————:".

The purpose of the first paragraph is to whet the reader's appetite so that he'll read your letter in its entirety and then your résumé. You achieve this by giving a brief overview of your background that includes one or two key accomplishments or responsibilities. Since this information will also appear in your résumé, be sure you change the wording so that you don't say the same thing verbatim.

In the next paragraph, you state that you're writing because you want to set up an interview and that your résumé is enclosed.

If you're currently employed, you may want to mention that you're contacting the organization on a confidential basis. If you feel that it would be advantageous to provide the name of your employer along with your title, do so.

The third and fourth paragraphs are optional. In the third, you would mention skills, strengths, or personal qualities you possess that are important in your line of work. In the fourth paragraph, you would mention an additional point about your work experience that you think might make an especially favorable impression. (The reason for offering this information in this paragraph and not in the first is to keep the first paragraph brief.)

The next paragraph explains that you hope to hear back from the person you're writing concerning a time and date for an interview or that you'll be calling to follow up to schedule a meeting.

The last paragraph conveys your appreciation for having your résumé reviewed. This expression of gratitude is a courteous thing to do since you're approaching the company on an unsolicited basis. No one asked you to send your résumé.

Here are two examples of cover letters for unsolicited résumés. The first contains the optional information; the second does not.

Troy Gardner
6 Melbourne Place
Palm Beach, FL 33480
(407) 582-6940

March 15, 1995

Ms. Billie Gates
President
Bonita Springs Racquet Club
2600 Country Club Drive
Bonita Springs, FL 33923

Dear Ms. Gates:

I have 14 years' experience managing tennis centers. My background
includes administering annual budgets in excess of $500,000,
directing staffs of up to 23 people, and dramatically increasing
clubs' profits and membership.

I'm writing you because I'm exploring on a confidential basis
opportunities outside of The Palm Beach Tennis Center, where I'm
General Manager/Director of Tennis. I would like to meet with you in
person to discuss how my background might be of value to Bonita
Springs. My résumé is enclosed for your review.

I have an excellent reputation as a manager, instructor, and player.
With outstanding human relations skills, I combine the management
knowledge, resourcefulness, and inexhaustible enthusiasm that are
necessary for planning and executing a topflight tennis operation.

In addition to my day-to-day management responsibilities, I'm also a
consultant to the Professional Golf Association. Here, I provide
expertise in all areas of tennis operations, court construction, and
maintenance, as well as the evaluation and review of tennis
facilities throughout the P.G.A. network.

I hope my background is of interest to you and that I hear from you
concerning a time and date for an interview.

Thank you in advance for reviewing my résumé.

Very truly yours,

Troy Gardner

Brenda Slayton
43 El Camino Real
Sarasota, FL 34242
(813) 346-9041

January 4, 1996

Mr. Bill Nelson
National Sales Manager
Apex Surgical Supplies, Inc.
2300 Industrial Boulevard
Dallas, TX 75241

Dear Mr. Nelson:

I have 8 years' experience selling medical supplies to hospitals. In this period of time, I've increased sales in my territory from $200,000 to over $1,500,000. The number of accounts has grown from 8 to 62. In addition, I've consistently been one of the top producers in the company out of 60 sales reps nationwide: #12 in 1993, #6 in 1994, and #2 in 1995.

I'm writing you because I'd like to meet with you to discuss employment opportunities at your company. My résumé is enclosed for your review.

I will give you a call early next week to see if we can schedule an appointment.

Thank you in advance for reviewing my background.

Very truly yours,

Brenda Slayton

If you happen to be knowledgeable about a company you're writing to, say something to this effect in the cover letter. This will show that you're not contacting the organization at random, but, instead, have a particular reason for wanting to explore employment opportunities with the organization. Here's an example:

Philip Barrington
16 Exeter Place
Sarasota, FL 34233
(813) 925-4502

January 12, 1996

Mr. Steve Holt
Vice President-Manufacturing
Holt Industries, Inc.
25 Commerce Drive
Tampa, FL 33609

Dear Mr. Holt:

I've been following your company for several years and am extremely impressed with not only your growth but also two of your policies: (1) building a product line that consists of products that are difficult to manufacture, and (2) utilizing the work-team approach instead of the traditional hierarchical style of management. I would very much like to meet with you to discuss employment opportunities at Holt Industries.

As my enclosed résumé explains, I have a B.S. degree in manufacturing engineering plus extensive experience in R.F. heat-sealing operations. My background includes introducing new products into production as well as designing new production machinery and processes. I'm particularly proud of my track record of having devised manufacturing methods that have dramatically increased output while reducing production time.

I hope you find my experience to be of interest to Holt Industries. I will give you a call in a few days to see if we can schedule a time to meet.

Thank you in advance for considering my background.

Sincerely,

Philip Barrington

In the event that you're writing to a company that has recently been in the news, a good way to begin your cover letter is by citing the article. You'll be demonstrating that you're interested in the company's line of business and also keep current on industry developments. Here's how Philip Barrington would have modified his letter:

Philip Barrington
16 Exeter Place
Sarasota, FL 34233
(813) 925-4502

January 12, 1996

Mr. Steve Holt
Vice President-Manufacturing
Holt Industries
25 Commerce Drive
Tampa, FL 33609

Dear Mr. Holt:

I was delighted to read in yesterday's *Wall Street Journal* about your
company's breakthrough in the design of the new vinyl inflatable
raft. This is an exciting product in a growing market. I'm sure
you'll realize great success.

I'm writing you because I have a B.S. degree in manufacturing
engineering plus extensive experience in R.F. heat-sealing
operations. My background includes introducing new products into
production as well as designing new production machinery and
processes. I'm particularly proud of my track record of having
devised manufacturing methods that have dramatically increased output
while reducing production time.

Holt Industries is clearly an innovative company that's on the
cutting edge of technology, and it's the kind of organization I'd
like to work for. I've always been impressed with your philosophy of
concentrating on products that are difficult to manufacture as well
as your utilization of the work-team approach instead of the
traditional hierarchical style of management. My résumé is enclosed
for your review.

I'll give you a call next week to see if we can arrange a time for an
interview.

Thank you in advance for reviewing my background.

Sincerely,

Philip Barrington

The ideal situation for contacting someone at an organization on an unsolicited basis is when you've been referred to the person by a mutual acquaintance. This acquaintance might be an employee of the company or a friend or business associate of the person you're writing. In any case, your first paragraph should begin as follows:

> I'm writing you at the suggestion of Steve McGrath. Steve and I were chatting a few days ago and I told him of my interest in changing positions. Because of my background in ---------, he thought it would be a good idea if we met.

In the next paragraph, you would briefly describe your work experience. The letter would then continue along the lines of the previous letters.

COVER LETTER FOR RESPONDING TO NEWSPAPER ADS

When writing a cover letter in response to a newspaper ad, there are two changes you need to make from the previous letters: (1) always make reference to the ad, and (2) state your qualifications according to the requirements listed in the ad. This may not necessarily be the order in which your accomplishments and duties appear in your résumé.

If the ad asks for any experience that hasn't been included in your résumé (and you've performed this type of work), add this information in your cover letter.

Many ads ask applicants to furnish a salary history or to state the level of compensation they're seeking. Don't offer this information.

You don't want to be evaluated on financial matters before you've had an opportunity to meet with a prospective employer and demonstrate your qualifications. If your salary is low, the company could doubt your capability and rule you out. If your earnings are high, you could be rejected because you would cost the company more money than it was planning to pay.

The fact of the matter is that if your salary is low, it might not be a true indicator of your ability. You could be working for an organization that has a low pay scale but offers an outstanding fringe benefits package. If your salary is high, you could possess certain skills and abilities that the company wasn't expecting you to have but would gladly pay for once it met you.

Studies have been conducted on companies' requests for salary information and job hunters' responses. The findings have been that most individuals don't provide the information asked for and few companies pass up qualified applicants as a result.

Occasionally, you might lose out on an interview because you didn't comply with a company's request. This will be more than offset by the advantages you'll realize by not discussing compensation.

If you see an ad you want to answer and the ad asks for salary information, conclude your cover letter by stating "I will be pleased to discuss compensation once a mutual interest has been established." This way you're acknowledging the company's request and not being rude by ignoring it.

Here's an example of an ad and the cover letter that was sent in response to it. Notice how the information provided in the letter parallels the experience asked for in the ad.

HIGH NET WORTH SALES MANAGER

Continental Bank seeks a seasoned professional to manage and direct the High Net Worth Sales group. This Boston-based position will require incumbent to orchestrate a corporate-wide sales effort dedicated to the development of new business from High Net Worth clients and prospects. The incumbent will develop annual business plans, manage a professional business development staff, build annual budget, and set asset and profit goals. The person we seek must be able to successfully manage and cultivate referrals with Personal Trust, Private Banking, Community Banking, Commercial Banking and National Banking Group. Superb presentation and leadership skills essential. 10+ years' experience in a related field required. Demonstrated ability to build and grow High Net Worth Sales effort necessary.

Respond to Dan Hollingsworth, Vice President-Human Resources, Continental Bank Corp., One State St., Boston, MA, 02211.

Jerry Greenwald
100 W. Flagler St.
Miami, FL 33130
(305) 375-6178

October 27, 1995

Mr. Dan Hollingsworth
Vice President-Human Resources
Continental Bank Corp.
One State St.
Boston, MA 02211

Dear Mr. Hollingsworth:

This is in response to your *New York Times* advertisement of October 22 for a "High Net Worth Sales Manager."

As my enclosed résumé explains, I have 20+ years' experience in Trust and Investment Division Management. My background includes establishing trust departments, hiring, training, and managing the sales staff, plus complete responsibility for business planning, budgeting, goal-setting, and all sales/marketing programs leading to new trust and investment management business with high net worth individuals and families. I am particularly proud of my accomplishments in the areas of seminar design and presentation plus my ability to cultivate internal and external referrals. I currently direct a department that has trust assets under management in excess of $900,000,000.

I would like to explore the "High Net Worth Sales Manager" position with you. I am confident that I possess the vision, resourcefulness, and stamina required to make the group an extraordinary success.

Having grown up in Waltham and graduated from Waltham High School, I have family and friends in the Boston area, which my wife and I visit regularly.

Sincerely,

Jerry Greenwald

If you're fortunate enough to know someone at the company that's doing the advertising, speak with this person and ask if you may use his name in your cover letter. In this situation, Jerry Greenwald's opening paragraph would have been as follows:

```
This is in response to your New York Times advertisement
of October 22 for a "High Net Worth Sales Manager."
Margaret Stahl of your Consumer Loans Department, whom
I've known for for over 5 years, told me about the posi-
tion and encouraged me to contact you.
```

This referral will give you a great deal of credibility and increase the likelihood of being interviewed, especially if your contact will be speaking on your behalf to the person you're writing.

COVER LETTER FOR CONTACTING EXECUTIVE SEARCH FIRMS

If you'll be sending your résumé to executive search firms, the cover letter you'll use will be almost identical to the one for contacting companies on an unsolicited basis. There are two significant differences, however.

First, you need not write to someone by name and title. Although this is the preferred approach, it's acceptable to begin with "Dear Sir or Madam." Second, feel free to give recruiters guidelines for the type of opportunity you're seeking. Your requirements could pertain to the position, the type of organization you want to join, or the geographic area you prefer. Here's how Troy Gardner would have modified his letter for sending it to executive recruiters. Notice that his salutation is "Dear Sir or Madam"; he begins the letter with "As my enclosed résumé explains,...."; and he gives specifics about the type of position he's seeking.

Troy Gardner
6 Melbourne Place
Palm Beach, FL 33480
(407) 582-6940

March 15, 1995

Executive Recruitment Services, Inc.
983 Park Ave.
New York, NY 10028

Dear Sir or Madam:

As my enclosed résumé explains, I have 14 years' experience managing
tennis centers. My background includes administering annual budgets
in excess of $500,000, directing staffs of up to 23 people, and
dramatically increasing clubs' profits and membership.

In addition to my daily management responsibilities, I'm a consultant
to the Professional Golf Association. Here, I provide expertise in
all areas of tennis operations, court construction, and maintenance,
as well as the evaluation and review of tennis facilities throughout
the P.G.A. network.

I have an excellent reputation as a manger, instructor, and player.
With outstanding human relations skills, I combine the management
knowledge, resourcefulness, and inexhaustible enthusiasm that are
necessary for planning and executing a topflight tennis operation.

I would appreciate hearing from you when you're engaged in a search
for a general manager of a tennis or athletic facility. I would be
especially interested in a position that offers equity participation
or the opportunity to make a financial investment in the club. A
southeastern or southwestern location is preferred.

Thank you in advance for reviewing my background.

Very truly yours,

Troy Gardner

COVER LETTER FOR CONTACTING EMPLOYMENT AGENCIES

If you'll be mailing your résumé to employment agencies, you can use the same cover letter that you would use for contacting executive search firms.

While you'll make a better impression by attaching this letter to your résumé, understand that you'll get the same results from agencies if you don't use a cover letter at all. Agencies receive résumés without cover letters on a regular basis.

COVER LETTERS FOR NETWORKING

If you're doing networking and want to meet with someone for the purpose of gaining information about the job market or to generate referrals to possible employers, there are two types of cover letters to write. One is when you have a referral from a mutual acquaintance and the other is when you're approaching the person without a referral.

In both cases, it's important to make it clear that you're writing the person because you're looking for assistance with your job search, not trying to set up an interview. Here are examples of these two cover letters:

Armanda Sweeney
3884 Torrey Pines Blvd.
Sarasota, FL 34238
(813) 923-9927

January 7, 1996

Melvin A. Greenberg, M.D.
Chief of Psychiatry
Sarasota Memorial Hospital
1700 S. Tamiami Trail
Sarasota, FL 34239

Dear Dr. Greenberg:

I'm writing you at the suggestion of my internist, Dr. Arthur
Rushmore.

I have an M.S.W. degree plus 10 years' experience doing individual,
couples, and group psychotherapy. I have worked with both children
and adults.

At the present time, I'm conducting a job search and am interested in
affiliating with a psychiatrist who's in private practice or joining
a psychiatric hospital, mental-health clinic, or family-counseling
center.

I was telling Art about my plans the other day and he suggested that
I contact you and send you my résumé, due to your outstanding
reputation in and knowledge of the Sarasota mental-health community.
I would like to meet with you for ten minutes or so to get your ideas
on psychiatrists or mental-health facilities for me to contact.

I will give you a call next week to see when we might be able to
arrange a brief appointment. My résumé is enclosed for your review.

Thank you in advance for your assistance.

Very truly yours,

Armanda Sweeney

Armanda Sweeney
3884 Torrey Pines Blvd.
Sarasota, FL 34238
(813) 923-9927

January 7, 1996

Melvin A. Greenberg, M.D.
Chief of Psychiatry
Sarasota Memorial Hospital
1700 S. Tamiami Trail
Sarasota, FL 34239

Dear Dr. Greenberg:

I have an M.S.W. degree plus 10 years' experience doing individual, couples, and group psychotherapy. I have worked with both children and adults.

At the present time, I'm conducting a job search and am interested in affiliating with a psychiatrist who's in private practice or joining a psychiatric hospital, mental-health clinic, or family-counseling center.

I'm not writing you to try to set up a job interview. Instead, due to your knowledge of and outstanding reputation in the Sarasota mental-health community, I'm hoping that you might meet with me for 10 minutes or so to give me some assistance with my job search. In particular, I'm trying to identify psychiatrists or individuals at mental-health facilities to contact.

I will give you a call early next week to see if we can arrange a time to meet. My résumé is enclosed for your review.

Thank you in advance for your time and attention.

Very truly yours,

Armanda Sweeney

CHAPTER 7

THE RÉSUMÉ-LETTER

There's one final document to discuss, and it combines elements from both the résumé and the cover letter. It's called the *résumé-letter* (some people also call this document a *broadcast letter*).

As the name implies, this is a résumé that's written in the form of a letter. The purpose of the document is to present a job hunter's background so that it's impossible to tell what the person's age is, if they're unemployed, or if they have a history of job-hopping.

An example of this letter appears on the next page. The letter describes the background of Steven Jaworsky, whose résumés you've seen on pages 65–68.

①
Steven B. Jaworsky
15 Island Drive
Palm Beach, FL 33480
(407) 582-8976

February 8, 1996

②
Mr. Claude Louis, President
Faucet/Hopscotch Electronics, Inc.
20 Mosey Blvd.
Tampa, FL 33609

Dear Mr. Louis:

③
④
I'm the General Manager of a $2,200,000 business. In less than 1 year's time, I reorganized operations, increased revenues, and turned a $120,000 annual loss into a $100,000 profit. If you have a need for a strong marketing/operations individual, perhaps you would be interested in hearing more about my background. I have:

⑤
- Built sales of a computer-products company from $0 to $1,500,000 in less than 3 years' time, plus built an investment of $2,000 into a $5,000,000 audio-equipment chain.

- Implemented a product strategy to improve gross margins, which increased pretax profits by $100,000.

- Managed up to 10 different locations, a staff of 47, and the departments of production, administration, and sales.

- Developed and instituted management systems and controls that dramatically improved operating efficiencies and product quality, while decreasing expenses by 20%.

- Created successful marketing programs utilizing TV, radio, direct mail, catalog, newsletter, event promotion, and telemarketing strategies.

- Analyzed businesses and recommended sales, marketing, and operational changes that greatly increased revenues and profits, achieving sales increases as high as 50% in 6 months.

⑥
I was the youngest person ever to be elected president of my national trade association. I was also the recipient of the national award, "Distinguished Dealer Award for Consumer Electronics," for having achieved the highest level of customer satisfaction. I hold a B.S. degree in business administration.

⑦
I would be pleased to discuss the details of my background during a personal interview and will give you a call next week to see if we can set up a time to meet.

Very truly yours,

Steven B. Jaworsky

In reading Steven's résumé-letter, it's evident that he's an accomplished businessman, both in starting new businesses and in improving operations and profits at existing organizations. Steven gave enough information about his strengths and successes for potential employers to see how he might be of value to them and therefore want to interview him. But notice that he omitted the names of his employers, dates of employment, and the name of the college he attended plus date of graduation.

By leaving out these key dates, it's impossible to tell that Steven is 62 years old, a point he wants to conceal until he meets with prospective employers in person. He left out the other information—names of companies he's worked for and his college—just so the absence of dates wouldn't be conspicuous. By omitting these other pieces of information, no one would suspect that he was trying to hide his age.

All of these omissions, of course, are the very "details" Steven was referring to in the closing paragraph of his letter, matters that he would be happy to discuss during a personal interview.

The value of this letter is that it gives employers reasons to interview you, while offering no information on which you can be screened out.

You're able to get away with omitting this information because a letter is a personal document. You aren't bound by traditional practices as you are in résumé writing, where certain information is always provided as a matter of course.

If this sounds like the résumé-letter is a panacea for a troubled background, it's not. I'll explain why shortly, but, first, let's discuss the mechanics of composing this letter.

ANALYSIS OF THE RÉSUMÉ-LETTER AND HOW TO COMPOSE IT

1. Prepare your letter on personal letterhead. If you're currently employed, don't include your business phone number.
2. Always write to the person you want to meet by name and title. Never begin the letter with "Dear Sir," "Dear Madam," "Dear Sir or Madam," or "To Whom It May Concern."

    It's also best to write to the person who has the authority to hire you, not to a member of the personnel department. In the event that your background is so strong that you think you might be viewed as a competitive threat by your potential boss, write to the manager at the next level up.
3. The purpose of the first two sentences in this paragraph is to give information that will make a powerful impression on the reader and prompt him to read your letter in its entirety.

You can state your title and responsibilities, mention a significant accomplishment, or both. What you say, however, need not necessarily have occurred with your current or most recent employer. You can state something that occurred earlier in your career.

If you decide to draw upon experience from a previous employer, it's important that you don't word the opening sentence so that it sounds as if you're out of work. For example, had Steven Jaworsky chosen to begin his letter by describing an accomplishment from his years at Profit Concepts, Inc., he would have written:

```
As Managing Partner of an advertising/marketing firm, I
developed multimedia and direct-mail promotional cam-
paigns that produced sales increases as high as 50% in 6
months.
```

By beginning with "As Managing Partner. . . ," there's no implication that Steven is no longer at Profit Concepts.

Steven never would have written:

```
When I was the Managing Partner at an advertising/mar-
keting firm, I. . . .
```

Starting the letter this way would have been tantamount to stating "I'm unemployed."

4. The last sentence in this paragraph indicates your interest in arranging an interview. Notice that Steven didn't write "If you have a need for a General Manager. . . " Instead, he wrote "If you have a need for a strong marketing/operations individual. . . " This leaves the door open as to the types of positions a company can consider him for. This wording achieves the same result as omitting an objective from a résumé. Of course, if there's one specific job you're interested in, then state this responsibility, just as you would in an objective on your résumé.

5. This section, a summary of your most important accomplishments and duties, is lifted from your résumé. Your contributions should appear in the order of their importance for the type of position you're seeking.

   So that this section will stand out and catch a reader's eye, precede each sentence with a dash. Also, when possible, begin each accomplishment and duty with an action word, just as you would in a résumé. If your background consists of administrative or support-type positions that don't lend themselves to visible accomplishments, list your major *responsibilities*.

6. This section contains additional information that will enhance your background. Topics to choose from include personal qualities, your educational background, and information that would

appear in a secondary section of your résumé.
  7. This sentence concludes the letter and reinforces your interest in an interview.

When writing a résumé-letter, try to keep the length to one page. If you need two pages, however, that's perfectly all right.

The résumé-letter should be typed or prepared on a word processor with a letter-quality printer. Use the same stationery you would for a résumé.

If your letter is going to be prepared by a secretarial service, make sure the style of type they use is Courier, Helvetica, or one of the Romans, in either 11- or 12-point size. Also make sure they don't place a secretary's initials in the lower left-hand corner of the letter. This might be suggested to you "to give your letter a professional appearance." What you want is for your correspondence to look like a document you prepared yourself and not like a letter that was typed for you by a secretary at work, on company time and at company expense.

SUCCESS-RATE OF THE RÉSUMÉ-LETTER

This letter was introduced to the job-hunting public during the 1960s by a new book that had come out on how to get interviews. Because the letter's approach was so unique, it produced outstanding results.

Today, the résumé-letter's success-rate is less dependable. Due to its widespread use over the years, the letter has become known as a vehicle for concealing liabilities in a job hunter's work history, and many employers immediately reject applicants when they receive it. Other employers, however, are not familiar with the letter, and they have a very favorable reaction upon reading it. They often contact applicants for interviews or for additional information.

Should you decide to try the résumé-letter approach, you'll usually have the most success if you write to managers and executives at small companies. Here, the likelihood is greater that they won't be familiar with this type of letter and they'll be impressed when they read about your background. At large companies, however, especially the Fortune 1,000, managers receive extensive training in recruiting, interviewing, and hiring techniques, and many will be knowledgeable about this job-search method. A good number will discard the letter as soon as they recognize it.

You'll also experience less resistance to this letter when answering ads than when conducting a mass mailing of your background. Many employers will assume that you're sending a letter instead of a résumé because you have a particular interest in the position being advertised and aren't necessarily conducting an active job-search campaign, with an up-to-date résumé ready for an immediate reply. Today, due to the downsizings, corporate restructurings, and layoffs that have plagued the 1990s, many people read the classifieds just to stay in touch with the job market. Their concern is that they have no idea when they might need to take action. Every so often they see an opening that really interests them and they write a letter in response.

CHAPTER 8

WHERE TO GO WITH YOUR RÉSUMÉ

Now that you know how to write a truly outstanding résumé—one that will highlight your strengths and accomplishments and eliminate or minimize any problem areas in your background—the question is how to use the document to get the interviews you want. Following are the different types of people and organizations you can contact. Let's discuss people first.

PERSONAL CONTACTS

Employment professionals estimate that 60–75 percent of the job hunters find their new positions through having a personal contact set up an interview for them.

There's a reason why this method is so successful. Whenever you're introduced to a prospective employer by a mutual acquaintance, you aren't regarded as "one of the masses." Instead, you have immediate credibility and are viewed as a choice prospect. This credibility increases the likelihood of both an interview and an offer.

In fact, no matter how glowing your references or impressive your accomplishments, nothing will mean as much to a prospective employer as the recommendation from a mutual acquaintance whose judgment he trusts.

As a result, when trying to get interviews, you want as many individuals as possible to be aware of your background and availability. There's no telling who might know of an opening for you or be able to introduce you to someone who works at a company you'd like to join. The more exposure you have and the more people who are making inquiries in your behalf, the greater the likelihood of developing meetings with prospective employers. If you're currently employed, you clearly need confidentiality about the fact that you're looking for a new position. You must therefore be cautious about whom you approach for assistance with your job search. Just be certain that you discuss your plans and show your résumé only to people you're sure you can trust, where you have no concern that you might be jeopardizing yourself with your current employer.

Here are the different individuals who might be able to assist you and to whom you should consider giving copies of your résumé:

Fellow employees
Former coworkers
People working at customers, suppliers, and competitors
Fellow members of professional organizations
Friends
Family members
Neighbors
Members of social clubs
Your accountant
Your banker
Your stockbroker
Your insurance agent
Your lawyer
Your doctor or dentist
Your religious leader
Civic and community leaders
College and high school alumni

When deciding which of these people to approach, take into consideration how much you think someone will be able to help you, not how well you know the person. Often, your best referrals will come from individuals you know the least. Many job hunters find that their best introductions come from business associates and not from their closest friends.

Editors of Newsletters

If your goal is to work in a specific industry, it may be helpful to contact individuals who write newsletters about that industry. These writers' names, addresses, and telephone numbers can be obtained from the following sources: personnel departments of companies in the industry, employment agencies and executive search firms specializing in the industry, and the industry's trade associations and professional organizations. In addition, check *The Standard Periodical Directory, Irregular Serials & Annuals, Ulrich's International Periodicals Directory*, and *The Encyclopedia of Associations*. These publications list newsletters and their editors.

Here are the different organizations you might want to send your résumé to:

PROSPECTIVE EMPLOYERS

Obviously, the largest target audience for your résumé is the organizations you might like to work for. To make a list of these possible employers, go to the library and use the reference books that list companies throughout the country. The following directories group companies according to product line and type of service rendered. They'll be excellent for identifying employers by *industry*.

> *Thomas Register*
> *Standard Directory of Advertisers*
> *Moody's Industrial Manual*
> *Value Line Investment Survey*
> *International Directory of Corporate Affiliations*
> Dun & Bradstreet's *Million Dollar Directory*
> Dun & Bradstreet's *Middle Market Directory*

To make sure that you haven't missed any organizations that are subsidiaries of companies, you might want to check the *Directory of Corporate Affiliations*. This publication cross-indexes subsidiary companies by type of business.

If you want to know which companies are the leaders in their industry, see *Ward's Business Directory*. It ranks 51,000 companies according to industry sales.

Guide to American Directories for Compiling Mailing Lists and *Principal Business Directories for Building Mailing Lists* state the industries that have directories of their own, including the names of the publications.

Another good way to identify companies in a given industry is to contact a professional association in that industry. Many associations publish directories that list their member firms. *The Encyclopedia of Associations, The Encyclopedia of Business Information Sources*, and *National Trade and Professional Associations of the United States* contain the names and addresses of associations throughout the country. Contact the appropriate organizations and see if you can obtain a list of their members.

A further way to identify associations is to call one or two of the major companies in the industry in which you want to work (the *Yellow Pages* will be helpful for finding local companies in that industry) and ask to be transferred to the president's secretary. This person will have the name and address of the national association. Also ask if there might be an independent association or local chapter of the national association in the immediate area. If there is, the secretary or president of that organization may be able to give you a list of its members.

You can also identify companies by *geography*. Use these reference books, which cross-index companies geographically:

Moody's Industrial Manual
Million Dollar Directory
Middle Market Directory
Directory of Corporate Affiliations
Directory of Foreign Manufacturers in the United States
Directory of American Firms Operating in Foreign Companies
International Directory of Corporate Affiliations
Bottin International Business Directory

The Thomas Publishing Company puts out regional guides that provide the names of manufacturers of different products located in various geographic areas.

Each state publishes a directory of its largest employers. The companies are listed alphabetically by city or town. (They are also cross-indexed by industry.)

The *Yellow Pages* groups companies by products and services within a limited geographic area. This source will be especially useful for finding small firms in the industry you're interested in. The directory you need might be at your local library, either the book itself or on microfiche. If not, you can purchase the directory from the regional telephone company.

A town's Chamber of Commerce will often have a list of the major employers in the area.

A final way to identify companies is to purchase a mailing list. Dun's Marketing Services and Standard & Poor's Corporation will compile a list of organizations according to your specifications for industry, location, and size (either in dollar volume or number of employees). Contact Dun's Marketing Services, Three Sylvan Way, Parsippany, NJ 07054 ([800] 624-5669), or Standard & Poor's Corporation, Dept. CDS, 25 Broadway, New York, NY 10004 ([212] 208-8300).

While compiling a list of potential employers, be on the lookout for companies that have announced impressive sales gains or have stated plans to build a new facility, expand an existing one, or offer a new product or service. These news items are usually the forerunners of increased hiring activity.

COMPANIES ADVERTISING JOB OPENINGS

Reading the classified section of newspapers and trade publications is an easy and effective way to identify companies that are looking to hire people with your background.

Answering ads should definitely be part of your job search campaign, however don't let it become your primary means for getting interviews. Companies advertise only about 15 percent of the jobs that they have open and bring in for interviews only 2 to 5 percent of the individuals who contact them because of an ad.

PROFESSIONAL ORGANIZATIONS

Professional organizations schedule meetings on a regular basis—often monthly—and many will allow people to attend a session as a guest. This is a wonderful way to network and get to know individuals who work in a particular field or industry.

Many of these organizations schedule time for networking before the meeting actually begins. Therefore bring an ample supply of résumés with you.

Be judicious, however, about how many copies you hand out and how aggressively you approach people to discuss your current situation. You don't want to appear desperate in your search for a job. You can always chat with someone, get their name along with the name of their employer, and then call them a few days later to set up a lunch date.

EXECUTIVE SEARCH FIRMS

If you're a manager earning in the area of $75,000 a year or more, sending your résumé to executive recruiters is essential. It's estimated that companies fill 25 percent of their management-level openings through these organizations.

To identify executive search firms, purchase a copy of the *Directory of Executive Recruiters*. This reference book lists firms throughout the country, including the minimum salary levels at which they work and the industries and job functions in which they specialize. The publication also cross-indexes search firms by industry and job function. You can buy a copy from Kennedy Publications, 2 Kennedy Way, Fitzwilliam, NH 03447 ([800] 531-0007).

Another excellent source for locating search firms is *The Recruiting & Search Report*. There are four regional editions, with groupings according to industry and job function. Write to or call P.O. Box 9433, Panama City Beach, FL 32417 ([800] 634-4548).

In addition, the *Yellow Pages* lists search firms under "Executive Search Firms." (A few of these companies, unfortunately, will actually be employment agencies.)

When contacting executive search firms, it will be advantageous to write to a particular individual at a firm. An outstanding source for the names of the top executive recruiters in the country is *The New Career Makers* by John Sibbald (HarperBusiness, 1995). This book identifies and ranks the most respected executive recruiters by industry and functional specialty.

For your convenience, following are the forty largest executive search firms in the country (this information was made available by *National Business Employment Weekly*). Most have branch offices in different parts of the United States.

Korn/Ferry International
Heidrick & Struggles
Russell Reynolds Associates
SpencerStuart
Paul R. Ray & Co.
A.T. Kearney Executive Search
Lamalie Amrop International
Egon Zehnder International
Witt/Kieffer Ford Hadelman & Lloyd
Ward Howell International
J.D. Ross International
Nordeman Grimm
Boyden
Gilbert Tweed Associates
Handy HRM
Whitney Group
Robert Murphy Associates
Johnson Smith & Knisely
Herbert Mines Associates
Norman Broadbent International
DHR International
Kenny Kindler Hunt & Howe
Goodrich & Sherwood
Diversified Search Companies
Howe-Lewis International
A. Davis Grant & Co.
Gould & McCoy
Heath/Norton Associates
D.E. Foster & Partners

Sullivan & Co.
Isaacson Miller
Daniel Silverstein Associates
Canny Bowen
Tyler & Co.
Christian & Timbers
Heidrick Partners
Battalia Winston International
Thorndike Deland
Barton Raben
Skott/Edwards Consultants

Since these firms are retained by their clients to find individuals with specific types of backgrounds, they will do absolutely nothing to try to set up interviews for you or to market you to companies. You should therefore contact as many of these organizations as possible that work in the field you're interested in. The more firms you write to, the greater the chances that you'll contact one that's currently searching for someone with your background.

EMPLOYMENT AGENCIES

You can either mail agencies a copy of your résumé or visit these firms in person. You'll find agencies listed in the *Yellow Pages* under "Employment Agencies."

If you want to identify agencies that specialize in a particular field or are located in a certain part of the country, buy a copy of the *Directory of Executive Recruiters* or *The Recruiting & Search Report*. These publications list the prominent agencies throughout the country, categorizing them geographically as well as by the industries and job functions in which they concentrate.

RÉSUMÉ DATABASES

An emerging job-hunting method is to contact companies that will take key information from your résumé and enter it into their electronic database. On-line clients of these firms will then access the database when looking for specific characteristics in individuals they want to hire. If you have the right background, you'll be contacted for more information and possibly an interview.

If you want to utilize one of these services, expect to pay an annual fee from as little as $25 up to several hundred dollars. What will often determine the cost is the number of job or industry categories you wish to be listed under. Some firms will charge you a one-time fee, entitling you to a lifetime membership.

A possible problem with this job-hunting method is its lack of confidentiality. Some database operators, however, will have a mechanism for withholding your name, address, and telephone number from their clients until your approval is obtained. Others will be able to prevent your background from being viewed by any firms that you specify. Ask which of these services are offered.

Since résumé databases are relatively new, and many have left the business after only a brief period of operation, it will be a good idea to ask the operator of a database how many employers are using it as well as how many résumés have been reviewed during the past 12 months. You want to be sure that enough employers are accessing the service to make it worth your while to join. Also, find out what industries or fields the employers are in, the size of these companies, and where they are located.

Here are some of the largest résumé databases in the country (this information was provided by *National Business Employment Weekly*):

Corporate Organizing and Research Services
One Pierce Place
Itasca, IL 60143
(800) 323-1352

Datamation Databank
265 S. Main St.
Akron, OH 44308
(800) 860-2252

Job Bank USA
1420 Spring Hill Rd.
McLean, VA 22102
(800) 296-1872

National Employee Database
418 Ashmun St.
Sault Ste. Marie, MI 49783
(800) 366-3633

SkillSearch
104 Woodmont Blvd.
Nashville, TN 37205
(800) 258-6641

On-Line Job-Listing Services

If you have a computer with a modem (or have access to one), you can join a service that lists job openings. Known as *bulletin boards,* these lists of jobs are made available by professional organizations, trade associations, trade publications, government agencies, college placement offices, and commercial electronic database companies. Many of the jobs have never been advertised to the public. They may also be located anywhere in the United States.

Sometimes there's no charge for using this service other than routine charges from your telephone company. Commercial operators, however, always charge an access fee. It's usually about $50 for a three-month subscription. Some organizations require that you be a member before you can use their service.

Many services specialize in jobs in a particular industry or field. Others, however, list jobs in up to as many as two dozen different categories. A few operators of bulletin boards also list jobs according to geographic area, and some even accept résumés electronically and then fax them to prospective employers.

Before joining one of these services, find out how often its list is updated. The more current the information, the less time you'll spend pursuing positions that have already been filled. Unfortunately, employers aren't always that prompt in notifying services that they no longer have a certain opening.

To get the names of organizations that provide these services, contact Coastal Associates Publishing, 1 Park Ave., New York, NY 10016 ([212] 503-3500). Each month this company publishes "The Computer Shopper," which lists bulletin boards throughout the country. These job lists are sorted by telephone area code.

Two of the largest commercial job-listing services are:

E-Span JobSearch
8440 Woodfield Crossing, Suite 170
Indianapolis, IN 46240
(800) 682-2901

CompuServe Bulletin Board
5000 Arlington Centre Blvd.
Columbus, OH 43220
(614) 457-8600

INDEX

Academic honors and awards, 13, 14.
See also Education
Accomplishments résumé,
76–78
Action words, 92–93, 97
Advanced degrees, 11, 13
Advertising, responding to, 196–99,
214
Affiliations, 81–82
Age, on résumé, 64, 170
Appearance, of résumé, 110–15
contrast, 114
equipment, 110–11
margins, 111
paper stock, 115
proofreading, 115
type style and size, 111
white space, 111
Aptitude scores, 100
Avoiding immediate rejection, 97–101
Awards, 13, 14, 83, 134–36

Background, 2–4
highlighting key information,
123–26
problem areas in, 19
Broadcast letter. See Résumé letter
Bullets, 93–94, 97
Career changer, 161–78
concealing your age, 170
partial, 173
Career history résumé, 76–78
Career summary. *See* Profile
Certificates/certification, 12, 84, 161

Chambers of Commerce, 213
Chronological format, 15–19
first draft of, 90
problem areas in, 19. *See also*
Problem areas in background
Classified ads, 196, 214
Clichés, 9, 98
College work experience, 86
Community activities, 82–83
highlighting, 165
Company-sponsored courses, 12
Components of résumé
education, 3, 9–14. *See also*
Education
job objective, 3, 4–7
key, 3
profile, 3, 4, 7–9
purpose of résumé, 2–4
work experience, 3, 15–22.
See also Work experience
CompuServe Bulletin Board, 218
Computer skills, 85
Conciseness, 91, 97, 99
Consolidation of work experiences,
102
"Consolidator," 26
Consulting, 142
Contrast, in résumé appearance,
114
Corporate Organizing and Research
Services, 217
Cover letters, 187–203
addressing to person with hiring
authority, 188

composing, 188–89
for contacting employment agen-
    cies, 201
for contacting executive search
    firms, 199–200
for networking, 201–3
purposes of, 187
for responding to newspaper ads,
    196–99
for unsolicited résumé, 188
Creativity, 144
Customers' comments, 142–43

Databases, résumé, 216–17
Datamation Databank, 217
Dates of employment, 91
Degrees, advanced, 11, 13
Directory of Corporate Affiliations, 212
Directory of Executive Recruiters, 214,
    216
Diversity in background, 69
Dun's Marketing Services, 213
Duties, 91

Editors (newsletter), 211–12
Education, 3, 9–14, 89
    advanced degrees, 11
    certificates, 12, 84
    extra-curricular activities, 13, 14
    on first draft of résumé, 90
    grade point average, 13–14
    highlighting over work experience,
        161
    honors and awards, 13, 14
    specific background necessary for
        position, 9–10
    training pertaining to field, 13
Electronic databases, 216–17
"Eliminator," 43
Embarrassing position on résumé,
    40–45
Employer(s)
    emphasizing prestigious, 151
    identifying prospective, 212–13
    on résumé, 91
Employment agencies, contacting,
    201, 216
Encyclopedia of Associations, The,
    212

*Encyclopedia of Business Information
    Sources*, 212
Entry-level positions, broad objectives
    and, 7. *See also* Graduating student
E-Span Job Search, 218
Executive search firms, contacting,
    199–200, 214–16
Experience, 3, 15–22
    chronological format, 15–19
    functional format, 19–22

First draft, 90
Foreign languages, 85
Functional format, 15, 19–22
    "Consolidator," 26
    de-emphasizing background prob-
        lem areas in, 19. *See also* Problem
        areas in background
    drawbacks to, 79–80
    "Eliminator," 43
    headings, 96
    "Magnet," 32
    "Minimizer," 46, 55
    "Stabilizer," 37

Generalities, 6
Geography, identifying companies by,
    213
Goal-directed applicants, 4
Grade point average, 13–14, 100
Graduating student, 179–82
Graduation date, 170
*Guide to American Directories for
    Compiling Mailing Lists*, 212

High school education, 12
Hobbies, 86
Honors, 13, 14, 83, 134–36
Housewife reentering work force,
    183–86
Hype, 9

"I," use of, 92, 98
Industry leaders, identifying, 212
Interests, 86
Irregular Serials & Annuals, 212

Job Bank USA, 217
Job-hopping, 52–57

Job objective, 3, 4–7
  wording, 5–7
Job title, 91

Key background information, highlighting, 123–26

Laser printing, 110–11
Lectures, 12
Length, of résumé, 101–10
Letterhead, 90, 206
Letters of recommendation, 140–41.
  See also References
Licenses, 84

"Magnet," 32
Mailing lists, 212, 213
Margins, 111
Marital status, 100
Marketing, 142–43
Memberships, 81–82, 100
Military experience, 86–88
"Minimizer," 46, 55
Misrepresentation, 64
Multiple strengths, conveying, 117–18
Mutual acquaintances, 196, 210
"My," use of, 98
Mystique, creating, 95

National Business Employment Weekly,
  58, 215, 217
National Employee Database, 217
*National Trade and Professional
  Associations of the United States*, 212
Networking, 201–3
New Career Makers, The, 215
Newsletter editors, 211–12
Newspaper ads, responding to, 196–99
Numbers, to convey extent of experi-
  ence, 93

Objective, 3, 4–7
  vs. profile, 89
  /profile combination, 132–33
  wording, 5–7
On-line job-listing services, 218

Paper stock, 115
Part-time jobs, 86

Patents, 84
Personal contacts, 210–11
Personal data, 88, 100
Personal qualities, highlighting important, 130–31
Personnel departments, contacting,
  188
Photograph, enclosing with résumé,
  100
Prestigious companies, 151
*Principal Business Directories for Building
  Mailing Lists*, 212
Printing equipment, 110–11
Problem areas in background
  being unemployed, 58–64
  embarrassing position on résumé,
    40–45
  history of unrelated positions,
    23–28
  lack of traditional experience in the
    position, 29–33
  listed, 19
  nearing retirement age, 64–69
  recent decrease in responsibility,
    34–39
  record of job-hopping, 52–57
  several periods of unemployment,
    46–51
Product knowledge, 96
Professional associations, 212
Professional experience/background.
  See Work Experience
Professional organizations, 81–82, 214
Profile, 3, 4, 7–9, 90, 116–31
  avoiding clichés in, 98
  early work experience, highlighting,
    127–29
  examples, 8–9
  key background information, high-
    lighting, 123–26
  multiple strengths, conveying,
    117–18
  vs. objective, 89
  objective/profile combination,
    132–33
  personal qualities, highlighting
    important, 130–31
  qualifications for diverse job objec-
    tive, conveying, 119–22

Proofreading, 115
Prospective employers, contacting,
    212–13
Psychological test results, 100
Publications, 84–85
Purpose, of résumé, 2–4

Qualifications
    for diverse job objective, conveying,
        119–22
    presenting, 2–4

Recommendation, letters of, 140–41
Recruiting & Search Report, The, 214–15,
    216
Recruitment, 137–39, 199–200, 214–16
References, 101. See also
        Recommendation, letters of
Rejection, avoiding immediate,
    97–101
Relocation, 100–101
Repetition
    of positions, 157
    in wording on résumé, 99
Responsibility
    decrease in, 34–39
    progression of increase in, 154–56
Résumé databases, 216–17
Résumé-interview ratio, 1
Résumé letter, 69, 204–9
    analysis and composition of, 206–8
    success rate of, 208–9

Salary history, 101, 196
Secondary sections, 81–88, 89
    community activities, 82–83
    computer skills, 85
    on first draft, 90
    foreign languages, 85
    hobbies and interests, 86
    honors and awards, 83
    licenses and certifications, 84
    military experience, 86–88
    part-time jobs and college work
        experience, 86
    patents, 84
    personal data, 88
    professional organizations, 81–82
    publications, 84–85

Seminars, 12
Senior-level job hunters
    profile of, 7
Sibbald, John, 215
Skills, highlighting, 163
SkillSearch, 217
Special job hunters, 161–86
    career changer, 161–78
    graduating student, 179–82
    housewife reentering work force,
        183–86
"Stabilizer," 37
Standard Periodical Directory, The, 212
Standard and Poor's Corporation, 213
Summary of qualifications. See Profile
Superlatives, 9

Testing results, 100
Trade associations, 212
Travel, 100–101
Type style and size, 111
    for résumé letters, 208
Typing, 111

Ulrich's International Periodicals
    Directory, 212
Unemployment
    periods of, 46–57
    unemployed job hunters, 58–64
Unrelated positions, history of, 23–28
Unsolicited résumé, 188
Untraditional statements, 144–50

Variety, in language, 99
Verbosity, 9
Verbs, 92–93, 97
Volunteer positions, 83
    highlighting, 165

Ward's Business Directory, 212
White space, 111
Work experience, 3, 15–22
    chronological format, 15–19
    consolidating, 102
    on first draft, 90
    functional format, 19–22
    highlighting early, 127–29

Yellow Pages, 213, 215, 216

ABOUT THE AUTHOR

Born in New York City and raised on Long Island, John J. Marcus graduated from the University of Pennsylvania with a degree in Sociology. Since 1968, he has conducted contingency recruiting for Fortune 500 companies as well as executive search work, outplacement counseling, and career counseling in Los Angeles, San Francisco, Boston, and Florida.

Mr. Marcus currently resides in Sarasota, Florida, where he is the owner of CareerCrafters, a career-counseling and resume-writing firm.